What people are s

The Knowable God

John's Gospel is both accessible and deep. So a reading of the gospel that deals directly with the text can take readers to a good depth, without a fog of scholarly cross-reference. Peter Brain has done some weighty academic reading, and has learned much from doing so, but he does not flaunt this constantly. Instead he lets us encounter St John's gospel story, with its layers of meaning, its light and shadow, and its use of language, place and character to highlight the significance of Jesus. Occasionally Peter reflects on ways in which Christians might respond to the gospel and take its claims into their framework of faith; yet he does so in ways that allow us to make that response for ourselves. His writing style is articulate, logical and clear; he is a good explainer. This book arises from long and serious engagement with John's Gospel. It would work well for thinking church members – people who are educated, but not especially educated in theology – who want to use their minds to deepen their faith. It could be read for personal growth and interest, or to inform the discussions of a house-group, or in preparation for preaching from the gospel.

John Proctor, General Secretary of the United Reformed Church, formerly Director of New Testament studies at Westminster College Cambridge.

Reading John's Gospel can be hard work. Up close, it is repetitious and full of strange turns of phrase and detours that elude twenty first-century understanding. Peter Brain enables us to take a step back and see the overall sweep of the gospel, driven by the passion of its author that we should believe in the Jesus who dwelt among us, one with the Father, so that his joy might be in us and ours might be complete. In this light, even the most troubling passages, such as the exclusivity of 'No one comes to the Father except by me' or the harsh sayings about 'the Jews', fall into place as part of a greater whole. Peter Brain's love for his subject is contagious. Having often steered clear of John to rely upon the more straightforward voices of the other gospels, I feel that part of the Bible has been restored to me, overflowing with energy and love.

Roberta Rominger, Pastor of Mercer Island Congregational Church (UCC) Washington state, previously General Secretary of the United Reformed Church

It's a lively, even entertaining, read. Thought-provoking and, without losing its serious purpose, it has sufficient contemporary images and verbal squibs to make the reader smile; sly comments bring the text alive. ... The repeated emphasis on most Christians shuffling the pack of four Gospels so that the different emphases of each are lost is a valuable reminder to preachers.

Tony Burnham, one-time General Secretary of the United Reformed Church and Radio 4 broadcaster

A very enjoyable and cultured read ... This is neither a commentary or a devotional work but is a serious and informative mediation ... a gracious introduction to a distinctive Gospel.

John Sutcliffe, formerly General Secretary of the Christian Education Movement

The
Knowable God

A fresh look at the Fourth Gospel

The
Knowable God

A fresh look at the Fourth Gospel

Peter Brain

Winchester, UK
Washington, USA

First published by Circle Books, 2019
Circle Books is an imprint of John Hunt Publishing Ltd., No. 3 East St., Alresford,
Hampshire SO24 9EE, UK
office1@jhpbooks.net
www.johnhuntpublishing.com
www.circle-books.com

For distributor details and how to order please visit the 'Ordering' section on our website.

Text copyright: Peter Brain 2018

ISBN: 978 1 78904 105 7
978 1 78904 106 4 (ebook)
Library of Congress Control Number: 2018947613

A CIP catalogue record for this book is available from the British Library.

Design: Stuart Davies

UK: Printed and bound by CPI Group (UK) Ltd, Croydon, CR0 4YY
US: Printed and bound by Thomson Shore, 7300 West Joy Road, Dexter, MI 48130

We operate a distinctive and ethical publishing philosophy in
all areas of our business, from our global network of authors to
production and worldwide distribution.

Contents

Preface

There is something Wagnerian about John's Gospel. Not in the cast list or the plot, of course. But the way the Ring cycle is composed helps us understand what John is doing in his own work of artistic genius. Wagner works with a number of musical phrases ('motifs') some of which are a few bars, some only a few notes; each represents a personality or a theme or a thing. If you listen carefully, peering closely like an expert admiring the brush marks on a classic canvas, you can recognise these motifs, sometimes shouted by the brass or the chorus, sometimes whispered by the flute or a soloist. And then of course you sit back to admire the whole which is magnificently greater than the sum of its parts.

John too has a palette of motifs, some the universal themes of life, light and love, some the more faith-based ones of creation, incarnation, rejection and glory. The Prologue is akin to an overture (1 vv1–18) in which John introduces these motifs much as Wagner anticipates the subsequent music in his overtures and preludes. Within a few hundred words he takes us from the initial act of God in creation, through the story of Jesus and back 'out' to God, now knowable – and seeking to be known – as Father. After this opening, John's main supporting characters each have a turn on stage in the limelight: John the Baptist, Nicodemus, the Samaritan woman, the equally anonymous blind man, Judas, Caiaphas, Pilate, Mary Magdalene and Simon Peter. Each succeeding scene is constructed out of the underlying motifs, sometimes ringing out, sometimes barely audible; you do need to pay attention. There comes a point when they are combined at the climax of the story: 'It is finished' (19 v30) when one can almost hear the orchestra sounding off the 'glory' theme in the brass against the 'rejection' theme in the strings but all woven together in this masterpiece.

God chose Jesus; God chose to be Jesus. These two core

incompatible yet equally necessary beliefs are orchestrated and dramatised to perfection. And you can read the whole thing in the time it takes for one Act of Wagner to reach the interval!

Chapter 1

The Distinctive Gospel

In the year 64 AD the emperor Nero notoriously 'fiddled while Rome burned'. Historians writing several decades later – and modern historians too – differ on whether he was instrumental in starting the blaze, depending on their overall judgement on Nero and his reign. It is also uncertain whether he picked on the Christians to blame, though that would have been in character; such a persecution would have been popular. Whatever the truth, Christian writers assert that the apostle Peter was killed in Rome in the persecution at that time.

About 80 years later, according to the fourth-century historian Eusebius, Papias, bishop of Hieropolis in modern Turkey wrote:

> This also the Elder said [i.e. quoting someone earlier] that Mark, who became Peter's interpreter, wrote accurately though not in order all that he remembered of the things which were said or done by the Lord. For he had himself neither heard the Lord nor been one of his followers, but afterwards, as I said, he had followed Peter who used to compose his discourses with a view to the needs of his hearers, but not as if he were composing a systematic account of the Lord's sayings.[1]

Most scholars believe that Mark's was the first full 'gospel' written down in the 60s, and written for the obvious reason that the first-hand oral record, transmitted by the apostles and other eye-witnesses, would not last much longer if they were going to be killed or die anyway. To over-simplify, most scholars believe that Matthew's Gospel was written as a rewrite of Mark, arranging some of the material into sections with additional material, with the editorial aim of making the book more useful to the Church as a teaching resource. In that the writer succeeded and thus Matthew's Gospel is placed first in the canon of Christian scriptures – though some would say it is the dullest of the four! Similarly, though again not all scholars would agree, Luke set about writing an account of the story of Jesus, doing some independent research; he then came across the text of Mark and also some of the sources utilised in Matthew, and rewrote his draft to include lots of Mark and a fair amount of material shared with Matthew's Gospel. For these reasons it is possible to set down a synopsis of the first three gospels and they are often called the Synoptics for convenience.

The reason for this extended preamble is to highlight, as if it were needed, the fact that John's Gospel is deceptively similar and yet substantially different from the other three. As C. H. Dodd says: 'There is no book, either in the New Testament or outside it, which is really *like* the Fourth Gospel' (his italics).[2] This book, described by the author as a purposeful selection from lots of material, is 'written so that you may come to believe that Jesus is the Messiah, the Son of God, and through believing you may have life in his name' (20 vv30–31). It can be argued that the other three books were written primarily as resources for Christians or, in Luke's case, for those who were serious about becoming Christians, whereas John seems to say that he is writing for a non-Christian readership. None of them are biographies as we might understand it. John is the most evangelistic in seeking to kindle faith; his appears to be the least biographical in intent. In that sense it is the most blatant 'gospel' of the four, if by that is meant an assertive selective exposition of the saving power of the phenomenon of Jesus of Nazareth in God's purposes. John is 'preaching for a decision', emphasising the choices, light or darkness, life or death, truth or falsehood, love or self, acceptance or rejection. To paraphrase his conclusion: 'reader, you had better believe it!' (20 v31).

A second-century bishop, Clement of Alexandria, famously

said that 'John, observing that the bodily facts had been made clear in the (earlier) gospels ... composed a spiritual gospel'[3] as though the Synoptics gave us factual history and John added interpretation. Thus Clement began a line of commentators seeking to cut through the Gordian knot of incompatibility between the four gospels. There is hardly a village Orthodox chapel in Greece which does not contain an icon of 'John the Theologian'. And yet it is clear, and recent scholarship has been highlighting this, that the first three gospels are just as theological, if by that is meant that they were written to present and interpret the story of Jesus of Nazareth as the unique intervention of God in human history, rather than as straightforward narrative. Matthew, Mark and Luke each have a distinctive picture of Jesus which they are trying to get across. All four Gospel writers are primarily preachers, even if John declares his hand more clearly. None are biographers, journalists or historians as we might understand those professions.

Alongside his book *The Interpretation of the Fourth Gospel* setting out the extraordinary depth of cultural, religious and philosophical allusions to be discerned within the text, Dodd felt it necessary to produce his *Historical Tradition in the Fourth Gospel*.[4] This complements the work done by commentators in exposing the theological element in the Synoptics; Dodd argues that John's Gospel drew on a distinctive, no less authentic, source of history, derived from personal memories preserved through the oral tradition, telling of the life and teaching, suffering, death and resurrection of Jesus. Dodd argues for 'an ancient tradition independent of the other gospels and meriting serious consideration as a contribution to our knowledge of the historical facts concerning Jesus Christ'.[5] Indeed we would have expected someone like John who took so seriously the Incarnation, the down-to-earth identity of Jesus as the revealed Word of God, to take equally seriously the historical context, however dramatically and imaginatively he wrote up each episode. This is a proclamation of the Word made flesh, not some fantasy. It may be richly theological – that is John's primary purpose – but it is as authentic a life of Christ as that found in the Synoptics, not discounting plenty of editorial freedom!

Of less concern in this book are the matters of authorship, provenance or date, though inevitably they feature at length in formal commentaries. It is interesting that the oldest fragment of John's Gospel – indeed the earliest portion of Christian scripture – ever found was unearthed in Upper Egypt. The scrap of papyrus, now at the John Rylands Library in the University of Manchester, contains verses from John chapter 18 written on both sides (i.e. from a codex or book format rather than a scroll) dating from around 130 AD. This book was clearly copied and circulated very widely. Given that Egypt had a large Jewish diaspora, those who interpret John's evangelical emphasis as being primarily aimed at converting Jews to the Christian faith have some additional circumstantial evidence as we shall see.

Whether the book actually originated with John the son of Zebedee is a case made by some scholars and strongly resisted by others. There seem to have been several well-known Johns, as well as others writing as 'John' to add weight to their work, such as the later Letters or the Book of Revelation. This actually matters less when the underlying evangelistic purpose of the book is emphasised.[6] Unlike one or two of the Letters of John which are probably only in the canon of Christian scripture because of their presumed authorship – most scholars would claim that they were probably not so authored – the Gospel of John would have been among the first choices of any editorial conference, as it was when an agreed canon of Christian scripture was eventually prepared in the fourth century. And though a date after, say, 70 AD might seem to be required given the maturity and complexity of the composition, there is now no reason to argue for a much later date merely on the grounds that the author must have seen at least Mark's Gospel and perhaps one or two of the others. Dodd cautiously argues that his evidence of independent sources 'may rightly serve as a warning against a hasty assumption that nothing in the Fourth Gospel which cannot be corroborated from the Synoptics has any claim to be regarded as part of the early tradition of the sayings of Jesus'.[7] John himself admits to being highly selective: 'Jesus did many other signs in the presence of his disciples which are not written in this book' (20 v30), echoed in the postscript: 'There are many other things that Jesus did' (21 v25). Interestingly, Luke comments that 'many have undertaken to write down an orderly account of the events that have been fulfilled among us ...' (Luke 1 v1) as a justification for his own attempt to get it right!

All the four gospels are the fruit of conscious selection and editing, whether by one or more than one hand, and all are an impressive mix of reporting, imaginative retelling and underlying belief. It is not possible to compile a credible sequence of the life of Jesus without using all four as sources; indeed when Dodd wrote his *The Founder of Christianity*[8] he did just that. Scholars will continue to debate the authorship, date and provenance of this work, and there are several commentaries which analyse these points. But as John Marsh puts it in his commentary: 'the eloquence, nobility and persuasiveness of the story have not lessened down the years, for it is still the Gospel of John that speaks most tellingly to the simple believer and also most effectively plumbs the depths of Christian belief and commitment for the highly sophisticated'.[9] But this version of Christianity is actually very distinctive.

Chapter 2

Presenting the Good News

So what is the 'gospel according to John'? Is it the same as that discerned in Paul's letters or in the Synoptics? Obviously, much of the narrative flow is different but what is even more striking is the difference in what constitutes the meaning and message of Jesus, and thus of Christianity for his readers. It needs to be said at the outset that reading John alone will not provide an adequate presentation of the Christian message as preached over the centuries but that without his distinctive emphases the remaining Christian scriptures are certainly incomplete.

The reader will not avoid the conclusion that all that matters to John is the identity of Jesus as the Messiah/Christ. Other core elements in the Christian preaching, such as the ethics, the atonement, the 'last days' or the virgin birth, hardly feature in this presentation of the Christian faith.

Of the four Gospels, as we saw, John is the most conscious of his readers. This leads to one of the criticisms often levelled at John's Gospel, that it is too individualistic. The main walk-on characters are each given their opportunity to believe or not. Each of them is an individual but also a representative figure, standing in for a sub-set of John's readers, though the outcome of each episode is very much for each character themselves. It is all very personal, episode by episode, and the writer is clearly highlighting the need for a personal response, that response being to acknowledge the identity of Jesus as Messiah/Christ or not. By contrast, in the Synoptics, starting with his baptism by John, the message of Jesus is clearly aimed at the kind of national repentance and renewal as God's chosen people which characterised the impact of the ancient prophets; see Matthew 4 v17; Mark 1 vv14f; Luke 4 vv16–21. But there is hardly any of that in John. Even John the Baptist's role is simply to identify Jesus as Messiah and hand over his disciples (as 1 vv35ff). Thus, when the topic is supposed to be 'purification' (i.e. preparing the nation through baptism for renewal) it is the Baptist's relationship with, and recognition of, Jesus which is the writer's focus (3 vv25ff).

Though the presentation of Jesus as king is central (crucial, one might say) for John, the term 'kingdom' only occurs briefly in the conversation with Nicodemus (3 vv3, 5) and never in the public teaching of Jesus. In the Synoptics, by contrast, it is the core of the message; a word used dozens of time, e.g., over 50 times in Matthew. Jesus has come like a Son of David, to lead the whole people, to establish God's rule, to act like one of the great prophets. There are no 'parables of the kingdom' in John (as, e.g., in Matthew 13) and Jesus' descent from David is only a minor talking point (7 v42).

There is very little of what we would call biography in the four gospels and even less in John than in the Synoptics, apart from one odd mention of his brothers (7 vv3ff). There are no personal details, nothing about his appearance unless the remark in 8 v57 ('you are not yet fifty years old') might imply a face old for its years. Such matters do not concern gospel writers.

So it is perhaps not so surprising that the mother of Jesus is not actually named by John in either of the two episodes in which she appears. Up in Galilee she is at a family wedding at Cana to which Jesus and his disciples were also invited (2 vv1–11). There may have been local rivalry between the neighbouring towns of Cana and Nazareth which prompted Nathanael, who was from Cana, to remark 'Can any good thing come out of Nazareth?' (1 v46). 'When the wine gave out the mother of Jesus said to him "They have no wine"' (2 v3). Jesus at first resists her request in words which seem much rougher in English than in the original Aramaic, calling her 'woman': 'My hour is not yet come.' But he does oblige in what John calls the first of his signs. After that, unlike the Synoptics' episodes[10] there is nothing of Mary in John until 'his hour' comes (17 v1). Then, with a symmetry which is surely intentional, the second appearance of his mother finds her standing at the cross with some of her friends and family (19 vv26ff): 'Woman, behold your son'[11] he cries, referring to himself and not to 'the beloved disciple' whom Jesus (as head of the family) then commissions to take care of her.

If there is little about the family, there is also no treatment of the shared life of the disciples and, by implication, teaching about church life, which is a considerable strand in the Synoptics, especially Matthew – the only Gospel to use the word 'church' (Matthew 16 v18; 18 v17). The 'twelve' (never called 'apostles' in John) are not listed and their 'twelve-ness' – echoing the twelve tribes of ancient Israel – is not the focus of attention. Peter still features as the leader and spokesperson, but the other two of the core three with a high profile in the Synoptics and in Acts, James and John, are never mentioned by name.

Perhaps this mainly individualistic approach is why John's Gospel appeals to those Christians who regard the 'social gospel' with suspicion or even hostility. The transformation of attitudes and relationships, which is arguably the central element of the Christian message for Luke with its noticeable inclusivity, is not a priority for John. Nor is the building up of the church as such, which is Matthew's underlying purpose. The Pharisees are not rebuked for ignoring 'the weightier matters of the law, justice and mercy and faith' (Matthew 23 v23) but simply for not recognising who Jesus is. Though John is surely writing after the fall of Jerusalem and the last stand at Masada (66–73 AD) and these devastating events form the backdrop of fierce passages in all three Synoptics (Matthew 24; Mark 13; Luke 17), John seems to care little for such history. The end-times, which in Jesus' teaching in the Synoptics are (again with hindsight) described in terms of that catastrophic war, become for John simply an exercise of divine discernment of the true believers, who are not known 'by their fruits' (Matthew 7 v20) nor as those who 'are not weighed down with dissipation and drunkenness and the worries of this life' (Luke 21 v34) but simply as 'those who will believe in me through their word' (17 v19).

Often unnoticed, there is in John no expectation that Jesus will come again, whether 'in his glory with all the angels' (Matthew 25 v31) or 'in clouds with great power and glory' (Mark 13 v26; Luke 21 v27). John's 'second coming' is Jesus returning after the triumph of the cross, indistinguishable from the Advocate, the Spirit of the Father and of the Son. It is as though Jesus himself is now back with the Father, having 'conquered the world' (16 v33) and said goodbye – as at 13 v1. In Dodd's graphic words: 'Christ's death on the cross *is* His ascent to the Father and his return to His disciples after death, which is closely associated if not identified with the coming of the Holy Spirit, *is* His second Advent' [his italics].[12]

The nearest John gets to writing about the last judgement as others understand it is in the subtle asymmetry of a passage such as this: 'whoever believes in the Son has eternal life; whoever disobeys the Son will not see life but must endure God's wrath' (3 v36). The word 'disobeys' implies that unbelief will be evidenced in a lack of good works, but there is no scarier vision than that. The lack of divine love in a person means lack of eternal life, as we shall see. The 'last day' (11 v24; 12 v48) is presented in about as undemonstrative and undramatic a manner as possible. John specifically distances Jesus from the role of judge on at least four occasions.[13] Maybe another John (or someone taking that name) wrote the book of Revelation to supply the grand finale which the Gospel omits! But for the evangelist there will be no 'rapture', no 'end of the world': 'I am not asking you to take them out of the world but to protect them from the evil one ... As you have sent me into the world so I have sent them into the world' (17 vv15ff).

Equally interesting and controversial is the lack of any explicit doctrine of the atonement, as taught elsewhere in the New Testament and throughout church history. The death of Jesus is for Paul the moment of justification for sinners, the sacrifice of atonement by his blood (Romans 3 v25). Thus the Letter to the Hebrews speaks of 'a merciful and faithful high priest in the service of God, who makes a sacrifice of atonement for the sins of the people' (Hebrews 2 v17). But this is not John's theology; we will look at this in more detail later. As a trained Pharisee, Paul's preferred language is drawn from the legalism of the Jewish faith, with concepts of righteousness and judgement and sacrifice and scapegoats etc., although he seeks to rise above it – unlike later theologians who turned it into a highly structured legalistic framework of substitutionary atonement. But John is not tied to that way of putting it. For John the *identity* of Jesus is itself our sufficient salvation, if we believe that he is indeed the promised Christ. Yes, the death of Jesus was the death of the Messiah/Christ, an act of God, but only because the incarnation was the salvation of humankind. There is no sense in John that the death of Jesus is somehow an offering or a sacrifice offered to God as a ransom; it is all the purposeful victorious initiative of God's love from start to finish. And the believer can make this salvation his/her own, in terms of the life of the church, when 'those who eat my flesh and drink my blood abide in me and I in them' (6 v56). This is not the new covenant of a gathered company or church (or new Israel); the word 'covenant' is missing from John. In place of the institution of the new covenant at a Last Supper we have the believer's personal response: 'the one who eats this bread will live for ever' (6 v58).

Again, there are no accounts in John of the Transfiguration or of Gethsemane, episodes which for the Synoptics highlight the distinction between the human and the divine. Indeed when Jesus cries out 'now is my soul troubled; should I say "Father, save me from this hour?"' John's next words are very far from the agony in the garden: 'No, it is for this reason that I have come to this hour. Father, glorify your name!' (12 vv27ff). At which point the motif used during the Synoptic story of the Transfiguration is used by John: 'Then a voice came from heaven "I have glorified it and I will glorify it again".' For John it is the phenomenon of Jesus, the incarnation, which discloses and comprises God's plan of salvation. He will die like a seed planted 'to bear much fruit' (12 v24). 'When I am lifted up from the earth I will draw all people to myself' (12 v12). He will go and prepare a place for his followers so that 'where I am you may be also' (14 v3). The blessing is for 'those who have not seen and yet have come to believe' (20 v29). 'You must be born again. The wind blows where it chooses and you hear the sound of it but you do not know where it comes from or where it is going; so it is with everyone who is born of the Spirit' (3 vv7f). There is a single reference to the 'cup that the Father has given me' (18 v11) but it is not one he is agonising over in the Fourth Gospel.

These are some of the fascinating distinctive elements in John's presentation of the gospel. They are also some of the reasons why it cannot stand alone as an introduction to Christianity, not least because there is no emphasis on covenant, on collective or corporate faith in the public square.[14] Along the way, the reader seeks in vain for some of the emphases to be found in the Synoptics. There is no pleading with the Jewish towns lest they be lost and no sending out of the Twelve on such a mission (e.g. Luke 9 vv1ff); this Jesus is most definitely the 'saviour of the world' (4 v42) and it is the arrival of some Gentile enquirers that triggers a major pronouncement of Jesus' role (12 vv20ff). There is certainly no plea to become as little children. There are no sympathetic (or unwittingly prophetic) Roman centurions; there is no Herod, no Zacchaeus, no rich young ruler, no feast in the house of Levi, no triple temptation, no Beatitudes, no Lord's Prayer, no Holy Week. Such differences are easily missed in our collective, undifferentiated memories.

The subsequent chapters will explore some of the events,

situations and personalities featured by John in particular passages, all very selective and deceptively different and yet so evangelically dramatic and persuasive.

Postscript: 'I AM'

The identity of Jesus is at the heart of one recurring phrase which John introduces into his gospel that is not found in the Synoptics – I AM.

At the moment of Jesus' arrest in the garden he challenges the assortment of religious and civil police who have come for him: 'For whom are you looking?' and they answered 'Jesus of Nazareth'. John continues: 'Jesus replied "I am". ... When Jesus said to them "I am" they stepped back and fell on the ground' (18 vv3ff). This brief but remarkable encounter has a key place in John's Gospel. It is the identity of Jesus which is at stake, and this is the core of John's message. Is this God in the flesh? In John's telling, this thought clearly crosses the minds of the police as they fall back on hearing what sounds like a claim. 'I am' (albeit, presumably, in Aramaic) is as close as can be to the ancient name of God 'Yahweh'[15] who met Moses and set him on the way of that first salvation, the Exodus, and which has been the holiest name of God ever since.

There are several so-called 'I am' sayings by Jesus, scattered through John's Gospel, each pointing to an aspect of Jesus' saving power through his identity. It is not quite clear that there are meant to be seven, nor do they fit tidily into a scheme of seven signs; maybe the mystical seven-fold pattern is largely there in the mind of commentators – who do not all agree as to which are the seven!

John teaches us through these sayings how we are to trust this Christ because of who and what he is. Two related sayings frame the other five, 'I am the bread of life' (6 v48) and 'I am the true vine' (15 v1). The two core elements of eucharistic theology, the remembering and the togetherness, are enshrined here. Though he does not recount the institution of the Lord's Supper, John clearly affirms the 'real presence' of Christ Jesus in the Church's most distinctive act of worship. Indeed he uses words which are, if anything, stronger than Paul's: 'whoever eats of this bread will live for ever and the bread that I will give for the life of the world is my flesh' (6 v51).

The other 'I am' statements remind us of John's 'Wagnerian' tendency, to weave his motifs into the story in different yet cumulative ways.

Twice Jesus says 'I am the light of the world', once during a controversy with some Pharisees who are challenging his claims and his judgement of themselves (8 v12), and once when he heals the man born blind on the Sabbath and gets into another controversy with the Pharisees (9 v5). This is a clear reference back to the initial affirmation by John that in Jesus 'what has come into being in him was life and the life was the light of all people; the light shines in the darkness and the darkness did not overcome it' (1 v4). The death and resurrection of Jesus is a victory foreseen from the start. And it is the eternal, divine nature of Jesus which is spelt out in another saying, 'I am the resurrection and the life' (11 v25). The same can be said of the great saying, 'I am the way, the truth and the life' (14 v6), which constitutes for John not three claims but one, even though it inevitably shapes many a three-point sermon!

Chapter 10 contains two 'I am' sayings: Jesus is the door or gate of the sheepfold and the good shepherd himself (10 vv7, 14). In both sayings the emphasis is on Jesus as the revelation of God, the point of access and the sign of love. In both paragraphs the contrast is with 'all who came before' and 'the hired hand who does not own the sheep'. By this time in the story it is clear that Jesus' enemies, primarily the Jewish authorities, are preparing to destroy him. John sustains the metaphor as Jesus confronts his enemies: 'you do not believe because you do not belong to my sheep' (10 v26). As the climax of the story approaches Jesus speaks of his own death as the good shepherd in terms which are distinctive to John. 'For this reason the Father loves me because I lay down my life in order to take it up again. No one takes it from me but I lay it down of my own accord. I have power to lay it down and I have power to take it up again. I have received this command from my Father' (10 v17f). For John the death of Jesus is the supreme demonstration of God's determined (and pre-determined) love.

These 'I am' sayings are one way in which John unpacks what he meant at the very outset: 'the Word was with God and the Word was God' (1 v1). There is no hiding the divine identity of Jesus. Greater than Moses (1 v17) he came in the name of 'I AM', who will lead his people out of captivity into the Promised Land.

Chapter 3

The True Glory

'There's glory for you!' said Humpty. 'I don't know what you mean by "glory"', Alice said. Humpty Dumpty smiled contemptuously. 'Of course you don't – till I tell you. I meant "there's a nice knock-down argument for you!"' 'But "glory" doesn't mean "a nice knock-down argument"' Alice objected. 'When I use a word,' Humpty Dumpty said in a rather scornful tone, 'it means just what I choose it to mean, neither more nor less'.[16]

A core theme for John is 'glory' – and it means what he chooses it to mean! He uses the words 'glory', 'glorify' or 'glorified' more than the three Synoptics put together, 36 times in all, beginning with the first, definitive time: 'we beheld his glory, the glory as of the Father's only Son, full of grace and truth' (1 v14).

Chambers' dictionary defines 'glory' as 'renown: exalted or triumphant honour' and also 'the manifestation of God to the blessed, a representation of the heavens opened' (as in the story of the Transfiguration). But though John knows of this given meaning, he plays on it to weave a different and distinctive interpretation of what glory might mean in this case. Though there is no suggestion that Lewis Carroll was aware of this (!) John does almost imply that glory does actually mean 'a nice knock-down argument' in Humpty's terms, since, for him, it has a distinctive meaning. It is the core of his presentation of what the person – and especially the death – of Jesus Christ means. We cannot read on into his book without watching out for this.

The Greek word 'doxa', which is rendered glory, started life as the noun from the verb 'dokeo' meaning 'to seem', sometimes as opposed to the reality, a superficial appearance which hides or even disguises) the reality. Thus doxa also meant conjecture, estimation or opinion, often in a disparaging way. But after the early classical period this evolved into 'outward appearance' which, when used of God in the Greek translations of the Hebrew Scriptures, came to mean splendour or radiance – a separately listed meaning in the lexicon. John's readers would have recognised the connection with the biblical meaning from the Septuagint (the Greek translation of the Hebrew Scriptures current at that time, probably produced in the third century AD). His central contention is that the human Jesus revealed the invisible God, that the appearance is the glory, the closest we can come to the reality of God. As Dodd puts it: 'This playing upon the different senses of a word is part of this writer's technique.'[17]

For John the most revealing action of Jesus as Christ is his deliberate death. In Paul's words: 'It is the God who said "let light shine out of darkness" who has shone in our hearts to give the light of the knowledge of the glory of God in the face of Jesus Christ' (II Corinthians 4 v6). That phrase might have been penned by John, though Paul, with the Synoptics, looks to the Resurrection as the revelation of glory, whereas for John it is the cross which is itself the triumph. John does not need a Transfiguration story; as Sanders says 'for him the glory of Christ was manifest throughout the ministry'.[18] As early as Chapter 2 for John, Jesus 'revealed his glory' in the first of several signs, i.e. demonstrated who he really was, so that 'his disciples believed in him' (2 v11). Unlike the glory of the Lord, sometimes veiled in the *Shekinah* cloud of the Hebrew Scriptures, this glory serves not to distance God but to make God known (1 v18).

But it is still the glory of the Lord, which had, for example, such an effect on the young Isaiah who 'saw the Lord', heard the angels sing 'Holy, holy, holy ... the whole earth is full of his glory' and cried 'woe is me!' (Isaiah 6 vv1ff). John has just told us that 'the Word became flesh and dwelt among us' (1 v14) where the verb 'dwelt' literally means 'pitched his tent' (in older versions 'tabernacled'). This prepares the reader for the phrase 'we beheld his glory', since it was at the tent of meeting, the original tabernacle, that God's glory shone out (Exodus 33 vv7ff) and Moses' face shone, as highlighted in II Corinthians 4 v6. This episode is clearly in John's mind too, when he considers how God was in Christ. As a king might send a prince who can act representatively on his behalf, so this is 'glory as of an only son from a father' who has been 'sent' – another favourite and unique word for John which he uses 40 times. For John 'sent' is not a distancing word pointing up the difference between God the Father and Jesus Christ the Son, but an assertion that God has not only chosen Jesus but chosen to be Jesus. There is no hint in John that this whole quasi-regal progression to the cross and beyond is not 100 per cent the initiative of God. Jesus' self-offering is a temporary departure 'to prepare a place for you' (14 v2), to multiply the effects of his one life since 'unless a grain of wheat falls into the ground and dies, it remains just a single grain' (12 v24) or again, 'it is to your advantage that I go away, for if I do not go away the Advocate (the Spirit) will not come to you' (16 v7) and, amazingly, 'that your joy may be full' (15 v11).

John describes Jesus' forthcoming death (not the Resurrection) as glorification akin to a coronation: 'when I am lifted up from the earth I will draw all people to myself' (12 v32) where the verb 'lifted up' is intentionally ambiguous, meaning both 'enthroned' and 'crucified'. In one passage John spells this out as fully as in the Prologue: 'Father, the hour has come; glorify your Son so that the Son may glorify you ... I glorified you on earth by finishing the work that you gave me to do. So now, Father, glorify me in your own presence with the glory that I had in your presence before the world existed' (17 vv1; 4). John's Jesus does not foretell his death as tragedy, with the promise of a resurrection to sugar the pill (forgive the metaphor) as in the Synoptics. The resurrection is bound up with the crucifixion as one wonderful and glorious event.

And glory is always the awesome power of the Other, never more than on the cross. For John the sun did not refuse to shine! Glory, a sense of divine wonder, constrains those who encounter it to worship, to do homage and prepare to obey, to seek pardon and to fear. It is a most tremendous concept. And yet, in Brian Wren's splendid couplet: 'We strain to reach your mercy seat and find you kneeling at our feet' (13 vv12ff).[19] John is not diminishing the awesomeness of God when he has Jesus redefine glory as love: 'having loved his own who were in the world, he loved them to the end' (13 v1). This love is now defined in Jesus' human life and the work of demonstrating it is finished (19 v30) on the cross.

One is reminded of the famous prayer attributed to Sir Francis Drake:

Lord God, when you call your servants to endeavour any great matter, grant us also to know that it is not the beginning, but the continuing of the same until it be thoroughly finished, which yieldeth the true glory; through him who, for the finishing of your work, laid down his life for us, our Redeemer, Jesus Christ.

Chapter 4

A Metropolitan Messiah

'After this there was a festival of the Jews and Jesus went up to Jerusalem' (5 v1). This matter-of-fact statement reminds us that one of the key differences between the Synoptic Gospels and John is the amount of time Jesus spends in Jerusalem. Reading Luke you would think that he made only one quasi-processional final journey there. This takes Luke several chapters to describe after the key verse when 'he set his face to go to Jerusalem' (Luke 9 v51) so that, on arrival, he wept over the city. To suit his narrative and his theological framework, Luke's account of Martha and Mary makes no mention of their home being so near Jerusalem – they live in 'a certain village' (Luke 10 v38). It is very clear that John is less interested in and less knowledgeable about Galilee, whereas his story has Jesus frequently in Jerusalem, including two occasions when he was nearly lynched before that final visit (7 vv45ff; 8 v59; 10 v31).

Commentators like to identify the sources of the Gospel writers in the period of oral transmission which evolved into written records. For many scholars, Matthew is traced to the church in Antioch, Mark to the recollections of Simon Peter, Luke to a less geographically focused research project collecting memories and especially colourful stories. As we saw, John was disregarded as a historian for centuries mainly because the theological framework and thrust of his work seemed to mean that he sat light to what actually happened. But if, with C. H. Dodd, we now perceive that John's book represents 'an ancient tradition independent of the other gospels and meriting serious consideration as a contribution to our knowledge of the historical facts concerning Jesus Christ'[20] we might reasonably assume from the internal evidence of the Gospel that the memories kept alive in Jerusalem were a major part of that independent tradition.

The Jerusalem church went through several upheavals in the first century. There was the violent early dispersal of Christians when 'Saul was ravaging the church by entering house after house, dragging off both men and women and committing them to prison' (Acts 8 v3). The initial sense of community in Jerusalem had included a sharing of possessions, in essence living off their capital and savings because the world was about to end. But this led to acute problems of poverty and weakness which Paul sought to address in his collection for the Christians in Judaea from the congregations which he had founded among the Gentiles.[21] Later the Jerusalem Christians would have been caught up in the Zealot-led uprising in the 60s, which led to the destruction of much of the city, including the Temple, by the Roman military crackdown. All in all it was an unstable half-century for Christians in Jerusalem, perhaps more so than in other cities. Then as the new faith became more established, into a second and third generation, the break with Judaism became complete and Jerusalem as a location became less important and their distinctive memories were almost lost.

But what seem to be authentic memories from Jerusalem do appear in John. As Dodd says: 'It would seem natural to infer that the milieu in which the tradition behind the Fourth Gospel was transmitted is to be sought in Jerusalem and the south rather than Galilee and the north.'[22] As well as identifying the home of Martha, Mary and Lazarus in Bethany, close enough to Jerusalem for Jesus to lodge with them, there are a number of other signals of local knowledge and memory. For example, he casually names as Malchus the high priest's servant whom Peter injured when Jesus was arrested. Significantly for Dodd, John does not name Gethsemane.[23] Again, on the night of Jesus' arrest 'Simon Peter and another disciple followed Jesus'. Since that un-named disciple was known to the high priest he went into the courtyard and a few minutes later 'he went out, spoke to the woman who guarded the gate *(fascinating!)* and brought Peter in' (18 v15ff).

In these verses there is no mention of Peter's north country accent, presumably shared by Jesus (Matthew 26 v73; Mark 14 v70; Luke 22 v59). John's Messiah is not in the tradition of northern deliverers of whom there were at least two who started out in Galilee claiming to be the Messiah, emulating the spirit, but not the success, of the Maccabees over a century before. For John the ministry in Galilee is secondary, as when 'the Galileans welcomed him since they had seen all that he had done in Jerusalem at the festival' (4 v45), even though the first formal sign for John is performed in Galilee at Cana. Later, after the great 'feeding the five thousand' episode Jesus was reluctant to return from Galilee, where he was relatively safe for the time being, but John significantly records: 'his brothers said to him, "You should leave here and go back to Judea so that your disciples also may see the works you are doing, for no one who wants to be widely known acts in secret"' (7 v3f). This is a clear contradiction with the Synoptic account of Jesus' ministry. Jesus did in fact go to Jerusalem again, though not with his brothers. On this occasion John records that some of the controversy around him was caused by his being from Galilee: 'has not the scripture said that the Messiah is descended from David and comes from Bethlehem?' (7 v42). John leaves it at that, as he has no real interest either in Jesus' descent or otherwise from David, nor in the nativity as such, whether in Bethlehem or wherever. The mood of the Synoptics, of a northern hero taking on a southern establishment (so vigorously dramatised by Dennis Potter in *Son of Man*) is quite absent, one of the sharpest contrasts between John and the other Gospel writers.

The Easter narratives are different not only because they are designed with a different emphasis from the Synoptics but arguably because they reflect other local memories. Nicodemus and Joseph are covert followers who are socially well-placed enough to approach Pilate, acquire the body of Jesus and embalm and bury it, temporarily, 'nearby' (19 v42). Then Mary Magdalene comes on her own, not to embalm the body as in the Synoptics, but simply to mourn; her first instinct when meeting the supposed gardener is to assume that the body has been moved somewhere more permanent. A younger disciple outruns Peter; that human touch is surely not an allegory of later church history nor a novelist's invention but a realistic recollection.

It is evident, though unremarked, in the Synoptics that Jesus has contacts in Jerusalem of which the twelve seem unaware. The use of the ass on Palm Sunday with the owner's apparent agreement and the availability of the room for the Last Supper, with a man carrying a water-pot as the signal, both point to more links than are spelt out. In the Synoptics the crowd on Palm Sunday are those who have followed him from Galilee, but in John it includes those already in the city still thrilled by the raising of Lazarus – 'the crowd went out to meet him' (12 v18). Of that Jerusalem crowd John writes that 'he had performed so many signs in their presence' (12 v36); this implies a ministry of more than those few recent days.

The most obvious and disputed historical divergence affecting the significance of Jerusalem is the episode of cleansing the Temple, which occurs early in John (Chapter 2) but in the Synoptics as happening during Holy Week, soon after the entry in Jerusalem (Matthew 21 v12; Mark 11 v15; Luke 19 v45). There is an interior logic to both accounts for the Synoptics, too, are writing theologically. For them, access to the inner court of the Temple (implying access to God) is a key interpretation of the Passion and death of Jesus. For the Synoptics this climaxes in the curtain which protected the holiness of the inner space being torn in half at the point of Jesus' death, establishing access to the place as a 'house of prayer for all people'. We have to forgive J. S. Bach for including this episode in his St John Passion when actually in John it is conspicuous by its absence! For him that curtain was torn in the incarnation itself: 'whoever has seen me has seen the Father' (14 v9). The moment of Jesus' death was not the enabling of access but the climax of the divine glory which was in Jesus throughout his ministry.

So when did Jesus 'cleanse the Temple'? The early stages of Jesus' ministry are set in the region of Jerusalem and Judaea, marked by his close association with John the Baptist which is described in more length and detail in John than in the Synoptics. The location of John's ministry is named as 'the other Bethany' across the Jordan (3 v23) but is unnamed in the Synoptics. The movement for national renewal which the Baptiser began was something which Jesus identified with, according to all four Gospels. But in John, Jesus' disciples are also baptising people and Jesus gradually becomes more popular than John in Judaea, before the popularity of the Galilean ministry. The gracious handover of his mission by John the Baptist is mentioned three times (1 v30; 1 v36; 2 vv28ff); he commends his own disciples to the new leader. In one reference Jesus appears to be consciously inheriting the Baptist's mission (10 vv40ff) but in a much more powerful and spiritually challenging way. All these allusions and little touches point to memories kept alive by those in the south, some of whom may have followed John the Baptist at first, as Andrew, Simon Peter's brother, is reported to have done (1 v40).

The account of the cleansing of the Temple in John 2 fits well with Jesus as a partner and colleague in John's ministry, sharing the Baptist's sense of crisis and opportunity facing the Jews. They were both impatient for change; the Spirit was moving and a crisis was coming. John offers us detailed touches such as the 'whip of cords' and 'both sheep and cattle' (2 v15) that have an eye-witness feel. John, as is his wont, continues the story in Chapter 2 seamlessly into commentary disguised as dialogue. But the episode does seem appropriate in its setting and if there is a possible Jerusalem source for John's material there is no reason to prefer Mark's timing of the story over this one.

Jesus would know that Jerusalem was where things had to be resolved. He moves inexorably to the main stage for the final drama of his last time there. If the Synoptics, from their sources, capture more of the feel of being with the twelve on the road full of eagerness and misguided optimism born of their Galilean experiences of miracles and popularity (most graphically in Mark 10 v32), John gives us the sense of how the Jerusalem establishment eventually could stand it no longer and moved in for the kill. Whether John or his sources had spoken with Nicodemus or Joseph, there is an insider's view which is occasionally evident as the drama unfolds. Compare John 11 v53 'from that day on they planned to put him to death' with Mark as early as 3 v6 'the Pharisees went out and immediately conspired with the Herodians against him, how to destroy him'. This time, one might say, it was seriously meant and Jesus knew it. We have an echo of this in Luke, when Jesus is warned that Herod 'wants to kill you' (Luke 13 v31ff) to which Jesus replies, 'it is impossible for a prophet to be killed away from Jerusalem' (though that assertion is of course not borne out in the scriptures) and then continues, 'Jerusalem, Jerusalem, the city that kills the prophets and stones those who are sent to you! How often would I have gathered your children together as a hen gathers her brood under her wings – and you would not!'

Surely we have in John's Gospel echoes of the personal experiences of Jerusalem disciples and of Jesus' ministry there. Unless we are already convinced that John simply let his imagination run away with him, we are being taken inside the collective memory of that first Christian community who 'saw and believed' (20 v29).

Chapter 5

Dramatis Personae

There are various ways of interpreting John's layout of the ministry of Jesus through the first 12 chapters, probably built around a pattern of seven signs. But the overall impression is of a sequence of significant individuals, representative of the categories of possible readers of this book, people who encounter Jesus and who are (or are not) changed as a result. The range of characters is as wide as that of potential readers. There is a religious searcher, Nicodemus in Chapter 3, aware that times are changing, that a crisis is looming for the Jewish people; he is sympathetic to Jesus and perhaps a supporter later (7 v50; 19 v39). There is an un-named Samaritan woman in Chapter 4, conscious of personal failure and hiding behind quasi-religious clichés, hysterically delighted to have a new start. There is a crowd seeking a political solution in Chapter 6, looking for a Davidic champion, who cannot accept a kingdom that is not of this world, as Jesus would later say to Pilate. There is an un-named blind man in Chapter 9, sticking to the evidence ('once I was blind, now I can see') despite all that the security services can do to dissuade him. There are the sisters, Martha and Mary in Chapter 11, representative of the questioning of mind and heart, both trustful in their own way. Through Chapters 5, 6, 8 and 10 there are the more or less self-confident religious authorities and their associates, learned in the tradition and the scriptures, who challenge Jesus on his claims. Like Nicodemus neither the leaders nor the crowd can see that God is doing something new, which is John's core message. And throughout it all there are the twelve, loyal yet fearful, those closest to Jesus but who, like the others in the unfolding drama, need to believe in the identity of their leader.

Characters like these, with more or less faith, have read

John's book throughout history and found that one or other of the stories refers to them. That is his purpose in writing; the stories are typical of the range of engagement required in Christian mission. Although the Fourth Gospel requires frequent re-reading to allow the subtleties and allusions to emerge – not to mention the theological depths – it is a book which can be a 'page-turner', full of real people, as inexorable as a classical Greek tragedy and as accessible as a novel or a screen-play.

In contrast to the Synoptics there are hardly any brief encounters with passing strangers in John. Each episode here is a set-piece, with time to do some character-drawing which allows the reader to become involved and reflect on what this story might mean for them and their life choices. Every character is drawn both as a distinctive part, *dramatis persona*, but also as representative of a class or group or attitude recognisable for John's readers. There are hardly any brisk parables and healings as we have them in the Synoptics. John's Jesus is more engaged one-on-one, concerned with showing how in dealing with real and recognisable people Jesus is bringing the living Word to bear on their lives. John always has the reader in mind.

Most of the encounter stories are followed by commentary, sometimes put into the mouth of Jesus as a monologue, sometimes disguised as ongoing conversation. It is rarely clear where the supposed conversation ends and the commentary takes over. Given that there is no punctuation in the original manuscripts, still less quotation marks, any attempt to highlight the '*ipsissima verba*', the actual words of Christ, as for example in 'Red Letter Bibles', is misguided. All the gospels, but especially John, put some words into Jesus' mouth which they know very well were not actually spoken by him but with no sense of deception. So we need to read the whole, quotes and all, to get the meaning intended by John as preacher and teacher. He goes to considerable lengths to unpack the significance of each encounter. The lectionary tradition and some daily Bible reading guides which present 'manageable' lengths of scripture, often do John a disservice because of the structure of his material. The Synoptics do not suffer in the same way as their episodes are generally much shorter; John's episodes are quite lengthy, sometimes a whole chapter.

Two examples of this extended encounter-plus-commentary are the episodes with the two unnamed characters, the Samaritan woman (4 vv1–42) and the blind man (9 vv1–41).

There is much subtlety and allusion in the story of the woman at the well. The reader will be drawn in by the sub-themes: there is the personal encounter of the Jewish man and Samaritan woman, i.e. across religious and gender taboos; there is the sensitive characterisation of the rather evasive and guilt-ridden woman; there is the surprise of the disciples who have been away buying food (which then Jesus declines to eat!); there is the joy of the villagers – all themes which might be enjoyed when the passage is read and then all becoming the reader's gateway to much deeper appreciation. With this story there is also a fascinating comparison with the story of one of Buddha's personal followers, presumably dating from around the fourth century BC. Paul Carus includes this story in his *The Gospel of Buddha:*[24] *ANANDA, the favourite disciple of the Buddha, having been sent by the Lord on a mission, passed by a well near a village, and seeing Pakati, a girl of the Matanga caste, he asked her for water to drink. Pakati said: 'O Brahman, I am too humble and mean to give thee water to drink, do not ask any service of me lest thy holiness be contaminated, for I am of low caste.' And Ananda replied: 'I ask not for caste but for water,' and the Matanga girl's heart leaped joyfully and she gave Ananda to drink.* This may indeed be a chance coincidence but it remains interesting enough for speculation that, as John was writing maybe in Ephesus, some travelling merchant might have told the tale and triggered the memory or the imagination of the evangelist. Whichever it is, our story is far more complex and profound than a simple lesson in the humility of Jesus.

The water in this story is symbolic as usual with John. In previous chapters John has told us that the water representing the Jewish religion must be replaced with wine (at Cana) and spirit (for Nicodemus). And like Nicodemus, this woman fails to grasp that Jesus is speaking metaphorically. Her wonderfully naive remark 'you have no bucket' allows John to repeat the teaching given to Nicodemus, namely that this temporary water will not satisfy and save, because 'no one can enter the Kingdom of God without being born of water and spirit' (3 v5). For the believer, says John later, 'the one who has bathed does not need to wash, except for the feet' (13 v10) as salvation is assured in Christ and needs only an ongoing spiritual life to refresh it. However dramatic the individual characterisation, for John the woman also represents her race. The five husbands probably represent the five gods which Jews accused Samaritans of worshipping, according to Josephus the Jewish historian. The actual city of Samaria was the capital of the northern kingdom of Israel after the death of Solomon around 930 BC until it was overrun in 722 BC by the Assyrians who repopulated it with their own settlers, bringing their own religions with their notorious five gods. The Samaritans reportedly mixed this pagan heritage with their Jewish one. Dodd comments: 'It was not in Samaria alone that a mixture of Jewish tradition with extraneous elements produced strange religious systems which competed for converts across the Hellenistic world.'[25] This woman is both a troubled soul and also a representative figure of all troubled and confused people who hang on to a tribal religion; she is dealt with by John on both levels.

As with millions of such troubled souls, Jesus has come 'not to condemn the world but that the world might be saved through him' (3 v17). At the end of the episode, once they have heard Jesus for themselves – though whether they overcome their feelings towards the woman herself is not recorded – the villagers (and, John hopes, his readers) can say 'we know that this is truly the Saviour of the world' (4 v42), the Saviour of all whatever their religious tradition.

* * *

The man born blind (9 vv1–41) is also a representative figure. As William Temple comments, 'The man blind from birth is every man ... and the Light of the World will deal with Everyman.'[26] In Jesus 'the true light which enlightens everyone was coming into the world' (1 v9). This man's physical blindness is dealt with in a way which draws out the parallel with human selfishness and sin. It is yet another plea by John for the Jewish leaders to recognise what is going on before their very eyes. This particular character does rather appeal to readers through the centuries, being stubborn and bloody-minded in the face of persistent authority, in this case the self-righteous 'jobsworths' who are acting like the religious police of some Islamic countries today. This long chapter is like a one-act play, albeit one in a sequence. Like the anonymous Samaritan woman the blind man is a believable personality and, like her, he comes to believe, i.e. to acknowledge the identity of Jesus. Like her, too, he is a representative of a whole set of people whom John wishes to reach through this book.

This story is an extended and dramatic presentation of the familiar metaphor of conversion as enlightenment which occurs within the New Testament and, of course, ever since as John wants his readers to realise. At his conversion Paul 'sees the light' in a most dramatic way on the Damascus road, and he uses the metaphor in writing to his churches (II Cor. 4 vv4ff; Eph. 5 v8; Col. 1 v12). It is ironical and depressing that religious faith should have been seen as darkness needing to be rescued by the essentially atheistic Enlightenment, the metaphor turned on its head.

Most manuscripts have Jesus challenging the healed man 'Do

you believe in the Son of Man?' (9 v35). At the personal level in the story it may simply mean 'do you trust me now?' but for John it is as usual more profound. Most scholars agree that 'Son of Man' was a phrase which Jesus used of himself; it is so prevalent. For all the Gospel writers, Son of Man paradoxically does not refer to Jesus' humanity but to his Messianic status as 'the one who is to come' (as in Daniel 7, vv13ff). The Son of Man has triggered the crisis; his appearance is in itself the occasion for judgement.[27] Thus John's story ends with the religious leaders saying to Jesus, 'Surely we are not blind, are we?' to which Jesus replies, 'If you were blind you would not have sin; but now that you say "we can see" your sin remains' (9 vv40f). This is an echo of the fierce comment of 3 v19: 'This is the judgement, that the light has come into the world and people loved darkness rather than light because their deeds were evil.' It is those who recognise Jesus as Messiah who can say: 'One thing I do know, that though I was blind now I see' (9 v25).

As this story begins the disciples ask a question, 'who sinned, that this man was born blind?' (9 v2). This is also a generic question for John's readers, an anguished cry arising in many different situations and circumstances. What of undeserved pain, suffering, disadvantage or distress? Who is to blame? Is that a meaningful question? But John's Jesus does not attempt to debate the question as such, but engages instead with the human condition, turning the question itself inside out. In other recorded teaching Jesus dismisses any causal link between good or bad character and good or bad experience: '... those eighteen who were killed when the tower of Siloam fell on them – do you think they were worse offenders than all the others living in Jerusalem?' (Luke 13 v4). So much for a 'prosperity gospel'[28] matching circumstance and merit. Interestingly this healing story in John is located near that tower of Siloam where memory of the accident was still presumably sharp (9 v6).

John Marsh wisely writes about this passage: 'no event in the past can make such undeserved suffering tolerable to the human spirit; only one thing can make it tolerable – what God makes of it when he does his work upon it'.[29] The location of this healing has a further significance for John. Siloam is indirectly derived from *shiloach*, a Hebrew word for 'send' (9 v7); the Greek word for 'send' gives us 'apostle'. It is in the continuity of loving and healing, commissioned by Jesus Christ, sending out the apostles and then significant through centuries of church life, that God's way of addressing apparently undeserved suffering will be shown, down to our own time.

Again John is addressing people who might happen to read him, those in darkness of any kind, even of their own making. This is the light of the world (9 v5) who troubles the comfortable but also comforts the troubled.

Chapter 6

The Knowable God

The popularity of walking holidays in Crete is understandable; the unique orchids and wildlife are amazing. In every village, thriving, struggling or deserted, the Orthodox chapel will nearly always feature at least one icon of John the Evangelist, alongside the usual set of Christ, Mary and either the local patron saint or the Baptist. And he is usually shown with the opening words of the prologue, for it is the incarnation which has been the focus of devotion in the Eastern Orthodox tradition since the very beginning. Yes, there are crucifixes, but they do not predominate as in the cathedrals and village rood screens of the western tradition steeped in its Latin-speaking origins. It will be recalled how proud Paul was of his Roman citizenship and of the system which delivered him to justice, which sent him off to Caesar. This background in the law undoubtedly affected his theology of the cross as the focus, the moment of salvation. He is the originator of the 'western' tradition. But across the Orthodox world at key points in various liturgies the priest or bishop will appear with candles in each hand, a set of three for the Blessed Trinity and a pair for the 'two natures' of Christ. The incarnation is absolutely central for John and the eastern tradition. There is a rather faint echo of this within the Anglican tradition when the congregation at the service of Nine Lessons and Carols will stand up out of respect for the final reading in which we are told, 'Saint John unfolds the great mystery of the Incarnation', as if now we shall have the earlier readings explained! The phenomenon of Jesus as a revelation of the nature of God is so central that a major branch of Christian theology, Christology, has been devoted to exploring across the shifting centuries just what it might mean to affirm that 'God was in Christ' (II Corinthians 5 v19). This attempt to express in words what God has sent in the 'Word made flesh' is the most distinctive and the most engrossing aspect of theology for all Christians, from catechumens to professors. 'No one has ever seen God – it is God's only Son ... who has made him known' says John (1 v18). But what is this knowledge of the unfathomable God, the good news which John is committed to share?

To begin with the context: all the commentators are clear that the Fourth Gospel is crammed with allusions to contemporary religious and other spiritual movements. C. H. Dodd discerns and writes at length about half a dozen, some of them very eclectic mixes.[30] Some scholars have held that this complexity and depth precludes the authorship of the apostle John, whom they suppose to be a simple uneducated Galilean fisherman like the blunt in-your-face Simon Peter. Maybe, but these echoes of diverse spiritualities are only the reflection of what was then going on across the Roman Empire at a time when that Empire was going through a period of consolidation, with more people able to move along fine new roads and share their experiences and beliefs. In many towns and cities there was a chaotic mix of old and new, the familiar and the novel, including the cultural inheritance of ancient Greek and Roman mythologies and more recent exposure to Persian and Egyptian cults, sometimes adapted like the various versions of Mithraism. There were also settlements of distinct faith communities such as Jews or Persians and even Asians. And latterly there was the importing by the Roman conquerors of an older tradition of deifying all-powerful emperors to consolidate the loyalty of captive peoples. Not only in Athens could a visitor say 'I see how religious you are in every way' (Acts 17 v20).

What anyone actually believed about the old Greek and Roman gods is of course uncertain, nor do we know what 'belief' might mean other than participating in the rituals and the companionship. From pre-history human beings have reverenced and sought to appease the 'powers' which apparently determined human character and circumstance, such as sun, storms, sex, drink, nationalism, creativity, etc., which were variously personified. That this was far from what was later called faith is clear from Homer, where these gods conduct themselves much like humans in a parallel but uninhibited universe. Traditional religious practice was (with doubtless plenty of exceptions) an accepted form of insurance, more a social contract, a declaration of belonging rather than a personal piety.

The contrast with the God of Israel could hardly have been sharper. Not for nothing is Abraham called the father of theism, of taking God so seriously that one's whole life has to change. Other gods would not have 'cared' that their people were in captivity, but the people who were later named the Jews believed that Yahweh, the Lord, first intervened to save them and make them his own. This was a living God, not kept alive by belief like the fairy Tinkerbell, but a life-giving, creative force able to change history. A few great individuals were in direct contact with this God and spoke on his behalf (hence we call them prophets), often in criticism and even judgement of the people and their rulers. 'Thus says the Lord' became the unique call of these spokesmen who brought the message. It was said of Jesus that he was a prophet, because he spoke 'with authority and not as the scribes' (Mark 1 v22). This has to be one factor in John's choosing the metaphor of the 'Word' to make his pitch for the incarnation. The writer of the First Letter of John[31] runs up the flag as he begins: 'we declare to you what was from the beginning, what we have heard, what we have seen with our eyes, what we have looked at and touched with our hands, concerning the word of life ...' (I John 1 v1). Couched in language which would have been familiar to people of many religious persuasions, John's Gospel is controversially staking a claim for the uniqueness of this Jesus as a revelation of the living God, the Lord not of the Jews only but of the whole world. And at the climax of his Prologue, grace upon grace, this is a knowable

God. And this knowledge is our salvation.

During the centuries between 200 BC and 300 AD CE what we may collectively call 'mystery religions' must have held their followers fascinated by the perennial call to be absorbed, even lost, within the spiritual reality of a greater presence. This involved a more or less demanding rite of passage and commitment to belong to the movement, occasionally assisted by drug-induced ecstasy. They all promised 'knowledge of God' in some form. Some added the promise of progress through life and beyond, in carefully prepared stages which were monitored and controlled by superiors in the order. This kind of movement, which had a long pedigree in Greek religion and blended well with some of the newer cults, seems to have been merged with selected Christian beliefs by a number of individuals and groups into what was generically known as Gnosticism – a term derived from the Greek word for knowledge, *gnosis*. This took various forms but in each case what was offered was salvation (highlighting life after death) through significant knowledge of God. It was against this Gnosticism that the apostles and their mainstream successors railed and argued for several centuries as a dilution and distortion of the true faith. Significantly John has Jesus praying: 'I am not asking you to take them out of the world' (17 v15) which is precisely what the Gnostics wanted. As Dodd notes: 'In the Fourth Gospel itself it is made perfectly clear that to know God is to experience His love in Christ and to return that love in obedience.'[32] Christianity insisted that the 'knowledge' sought in Gnosticism was far removed from that which was celebrated by John and declared to be the knowledge of God which is in itself eternal life. The mystics' knowledge was won by searching; for the Christian the essence of spirituality was thankfulness, the result of being found, a gift of grace. The Gnostics aimed to escape from 'the world'; the word ecstasy comes from the Greek meaning 'standing apart'. The Christians had a mission to engage with 'the world', for 'God so loved it'

(3 v16).

There are several discernible references within the New Testament itself to the dangers posed by these other movements of 'spiritual knowledge' to an authentic Christianity. In the First Letter of John this is spelt out directly: 'do not believe every spirit; [...] by this you know the spirit of God: every spirit that confesses that Jesus Christ has come in the flesh is from God and every spirit that does not confess Jesus is not from God' (I John 4 v1ff). This is the identical test as that presented in John's Gospel for true faith and salvation. John may be echoing or even parodying the language of a mystical culture when he puts these words into Jesus' mouth: 'And this is eternal life, that they may know you, the only true God, and Jesus Christ whom you have sent' (17 v3). This is a world away from the secretive, conspiratorial and inevitably self-righteous approach of the Gnostics and otherworldly mystics. Rather it is a spirituality of the here-and-now, an engagement with the world which mirrors the incarnation itself. Thus Christian mysticism is never an escape mechanism. Prayer in the name and the spirit of Jesus is *reculer pour mieux sauter*, a preparation for a fresh engagement with 'the world'. John is speaking of an almost unimaginable intimacy with the Almighty, as the French version of this verse makes even plainer: *'c'est ici la vie eternelle, qu'ils connaissent toi qui est le seul vrai Dieu, et Jesus Christ ...'*. Use of the *tu* form is a sign of intimacy in French which usually has *vous* for 'you'; and use of the verb *connaître* rather than *savoir* captures the feel of the original as it means to 'know' a person as distinct from to 'know' a fact. For this Christian knowledge does not – and dare not – claim to be any kind of *savoir* as though God were anything than the Other.[33] But it is knowledge, inter-personal, relational, a partnership or communion – far from a trance-like state. It is this relational heart of Christianity which John is highlighting when he affirms the actual involvement of God in our human life. The affirmation that 'the Word was made flesh' is one which is not found within other philosophical or religious writings or movements. Many others will agree that God chose Jesus but not that God chose to be Jesus. Christians will claim (pace Philip Pullman[34]) that Christ chose to be Jesus just as Jesus chose to be Christ. The incarnation makes all the difference: 'Have I been with you all this time, Philip, and you still do not <u>know</u> me? Whoever has seen me has seen the Father' (14 v9). As John said at the outset: 'No one has ever seen God – it is God's only Son, who is close to the Father's heart, who has made him known' (1 v18). This relationship is the believer's privilege, to know the Word, once made flesh, through the Holy Spirit and through him to know the Father and the Father's saving love.

Chapter 7

Still in the Dark?

In John Chapter 3 Jesus is in Jerusalem for Passover and he is visited by Nicodemus, a member of the Sanhedrin, the court of Jewish leaders. He comes at night, in a darkness which is as symbolic as it is literal – as on that final evening when Judas leaves the upper room on his deadly errand 'and it was night' (13 v30). This is a meeting which foreshadows – and for John represents – the encounter between Judaism and Christianity which dominated the life of the early church throughout the first century. Paul's ministry is shaped by it, often mired in the controversy with other preachers over how far Christians had to go in keeping the scriptural commandments and Jewish practices. Peter's 'second conversion' as recorded in Acts 10 is precisely on this point as he is reconciled to what Paul and Barnabas are doing in bringing Gentiles into the church.

John's take is in some ways sharper, which is why he can seem the most hostile to 'the Jews' of all New Testament writers, a very distinctive element to his Gospel. The old faith is so redundant that to follow it is to deny what God has now done; there is none of Paul's heart-searching of Romans Chapters 9–11 here. In the previous chapter as he tells the story of the wedding at Cana, John wants us to know that the Jewish rite of purification has been replaced by the Christian eucharistic wine of new life. John would never include the saying found in Luke (5 v39): 'no one after drinking old wine desires new wine, but says "The old is better"'! In the Synoptics there is a running motif that Jesus is somehow re-inventing Israel, e.g., by picking twelve disciples as apostles (Mark 3 v14). There is no such strategy in John, whose opinion (for it cannot be ascribed to Jesus) is clear that the old Israel has been superseded, replaced, discredited and discontinued. John's Jesus can say 'It was not Moses who gave you the bread from heaven but it is my Father who is giving you the true bread from heaven' (6 vv32).

In this episode Jesus is dealing with a representative of Judaism, a man aware of possible change as heralded by John the Baptist, yet loyal to his sense of belonging to God's chosen people. This chapter sets out a radical new beginning of which the phenomenon of John, baptising with water, was but the tip of the iceberg. Put bluntly, 'No one can enter the kingdom of God without being born of water and spirit' (3 v5). This somewhat intriguing and puzzling statement might be a fairly basic analogy with the waters breaking when a baby is born and the need to get the baby's breathing started. Or it might be a look back to the story of the making of Adam in Genesis Chapter 2 where we read that 'the Lord God formed man from the dust of the ground and breathed into his nostrils the breath (the word also means spirit) of life'. Or it might be an allusion to the two core sacraments of the church, Bbaptism and Eucharist. Whichever it is (and probably all are in John's mind) Jesus is speaking of a renewal of which Nicodemus understands nothing. He addresses Jesus as Rabbi but cannot grasp the new teaching. This 'spirit' (the word also used for 'wind' both in Hebrew and in Greek) may blow unregulated and unseen – how appalling for a bureaucrat, even a religious one! That some of the ancient promises were now coming to fulfilment, that God was about to do what was foretold, all this was profoundly unsettling and threatening. This thrilling sense of 'kairos' – a moment of opportunity – had stirred John son of Zechariah into action and led him like a latter-day prophet of the Lord to call the people back to their God and baptise them for a fresh beginning. Something was afoot and Nicodemus could feel it; but he could not really grasp it.

For Nicodemus and his fellow-leaders, the kingdom of God was something for the end times, beyond history at the final judgement. How could it be for the here and now? The phrase 'kingdom of God' may not occur very often in this gospel as compared with the Synoptics, but it is John's core message too as he develops the theme. As we shall see, the title 'king' is the crux of the dialogue with Pilate and is given to Jesus on the cross when he is 'lifted up *(enthroned)* that whoever believes in him may have eternal life' (3 v15). The motif of 'lifting up' has a double meaning here in Chapter 3, as elsewhere (8 v28; 12 v32), echoing the old story of Moses ceremonially holding high a brass serpent to bring healing and life to the desperate Israelites in their wilderness wandering (Numbers 21 v9), while at the same time foreshadowing the 'enthronement' of crucifixion, the glory of the Lord. For John the Jews, or at least their leaders, are lost in a similar wilderness, far from the promised land of God's rule of love. And this is to walk in the dark.

The metaphor of light and dark is perhaps the commonest in all religious writing in every tradition, and it is one of the core motifs of John in preaching the Christian faith. In this chapter, not only does the Jewish leader come to meet Jesus in the dark, but John's reflection on the episode compares judgement to the coming of light: 'all who do evil hate the light and do not come to the light so that their deeds may not be exposed' (3 v20). Even more sharply, it is for John the incarnation which 'is the judgement that the light has come into the world' (3 v19). He goes further, calling Jesus 'the true light which enlightens everyone' (1 v9). There is a universal relevance not limited to the Jews, a relevance by the time John was writing which was undoubtedly hastened by the rejection of Jesus as the Christ by those whom Nicodemus represents in this passage, even though Nicodemus himself became something of a supporter, if not a believer. There is little in John to suggest the possibility that, maybe even at the last, 'the Jews' (meaning the leaders, the establishment, the opinion formers, rather than the general populace) may accept him. This is in contrast to hints in the Synoptics, most graphically by Luke when Jesus weeps over the city which does not recognise him –

and might have done (Luke 19 vv41ff). John's Jesus would not weep over Jerusalem – though he is no less emotional, as at the death of Lazarus (11 v35).

Perversely, this passage is most dearly loved by many present-day versions of Nicodemus who are sure that God can have nothing radically new to say or do! But when read carefully it is quite a challenge to those who prefer to live indoors (spiritually speaking) and miss the rush of the wind, even the wind of change, which is a sign of the living Spirit. There is a risky and exciting inclusiveness in John for all who believe. 'Whoever comes to me I will never drive away' (6 v37) is a hard word to those who would prefer the frontiers of this kingdom, which they might define as membership of a church, to be tightly guarded (by themselves!). The various churches and denominations have always been, and still are, full of such would-be gatekeepers. The Jesus who talks with Nicodemus is a free-thinker, spontaneous and opportunistic, challenging the cultural constraints of his time. Those who follow this Jesus may affirm with Herbert Butterfield: 'Hold to Christ and for the rest be totally uncommitted!'[35]

But unlike some modern liberals John is not vague on the issue of that core commitment; he is forever preaching for a decision. We are to walk in that light which is the divine life and love; for John such a mind-set, with all its implications, constitutes salvation. This is a deceptively demanding message. It is far from the apparent security of abstract nouns or unfocused goodness which some call Christian values. It is rather, in the words of T. S. Eliot, 'a condition of complete simplicity – costing not less than everything'.[36] In Bonhoeffer's devastating phrase: 'When Christ calls a man, he bids him come and die.'[37] To follow Jesus is, for John, to walk confidently in the light of his truth and the glory of his cross, as we shall see in the 'farewell discourses'. Here, as one metaphor for salvation is merged with others in a splendid tapestry, John weaves his motifs into a presentation of great power. Compared with Paul, who only occasionally uses the metaphor of light, John uses it in around a dozen exchanges. And when it comes to interpreting the cross, the sun does not refuse to shine, as in the Synoptics, but surely blazes bright as the Light of the World demonstrates the identity of God even in death.

Thus for John there is no 'messianic secret' as found in the Synoptics where we read of the puzzlement of the Twelve when they are bidden to tell no one that Jesus is the Messiah, lest people misunderstand and seek to mould Jesus into their own prejudiced expectations of the Messiah. When, following the feeding of the five thousand the disciples are in effect called to follow Jesus afresh, the question put by John's Jesus is not 'who do you say that I am?' but 'will you also go away?' to which Peter answers not with a simple 'you are the Messiah' (which we know already) but 'you have the words of eternal life' (6 vv66ff). The meaning is the same but elaborated to fit John's distinctive message. Nicodemus and 'the Jews' do not acknowledge Jesus' identity, which he is not hiding. They will go on walking in the dark, and therefore in sin.

Jesus said to the Pharisees, 'if you were blind you would not have sin; but now that you say "we can see" your sin remains' (9 v41). That sin in John is wilful refusal to acknowledge Jesus as the Christ. Other so-called sins follow from that – there is plenty more about them throughout Paul's letters! But for John this is the heart of the matter, to recognise and to know, to believe in and to trust Jesus as Christ. Those who cannot see this, such as Nicodemus, are the ones in the dark. The light of the world, the 'true light' or 'light of truth' (1 v9) has come into the world, a phrase which Lesslie Newbigin used as the title of his commentary.[38] For John the preacher there are no shades of grey.

Chapter 8

One Memorable Verse

For God so loved the world that he gave his only Son so that everyone who believes in him may not perish but have eternal life. (3 v16)

This one verse, his best-known, beloved by embroiderers, engravers and sandwich-board men as well as preachers, seems to sum up the good news being presented by John. The overall impact is clear. Yet every word is resonant with inner meaning and subtlety.

Take for example the word 'believes' which is one of John's key words and yet one which he hardly unpacks here or elsewhere in the Gospel as though it is self-explanatory. The contrast with the Synoptics is considerable where there are many sayings, supported by parables, which spell out the practical implications of following Jesus and the very visible contrast between those 'believers' who act and those who do not. For example, there is a sharpness throughout the Sermon on the Mount, climaxing in Matthew 7 vv21: 'Not everyone who says to me "Lord, Lord" will enter the kingdom of heaven but only one who does the will of my Father in heaven.' Time and again it is simply not enough to profess belief; action must follow. The Letter of James, which reads in places like a commentary on the Sermon on the Mount, is fierce: 'Faith by itself, if it has no works, is dead' (James 2 v17). The First Letter of John insists on the same interpretation: 'Little children, let us love, not in word or speech, but in truth and action' (I John 3 v18).

In John's Gospel love is to be the hallmark of the true believer; but the emphasis is not so much on 'loving your neighbour as yourself' as knowing its powerful presence within. The love of God received through faith constitutes the eternal life promised by Jesus. For John the term 'belief' means not propositional assent to a doctrinal system or obedience to a moral agenda but relational trust in a loving Father through the Son. So he actually does not unpack the word 'believe', as is done in the Synoptics and in Paul's Letters.[39] John simply invites Christians to live like Jesus: '... the one who believes in me will also do the works that I do and, in fact, will do greater works than these because I am going to the Father' (14 v12).[40] To believe is to trust, to follow, to obey, to know. Believers are 'in the world' (17 v18) to be the harvest of Jesus' seed corn (12 v24). The life of outgoing love is implicit in a belief that Jesus is indeed the Christ.

Secondly, consider another little word, 'only'. The Greek word does mean 'only-begotten' as the KJV (King James Version) has it or, more colloquially, one-off and unique. In later centuries those charged with writing down as creedal statements what the church believed would agonise and split over this word 'only-begotten'. Things came to a head in the early fourth century when a priest in Alexandria, Arius, publicly refuted the claim that the Son was co-eternal with the Father, stating rather that Christ was the perfect representation of God but not 'of one substance' (in Greek *homoousios*) with the Father. Does not Paul speak of Christ as 'the image of the invisible God, the firstborn of all creation' (Colossians 1 v15)? This did not go down well with those who felt that Arius was diluting the presence of God in the life and death of Jesus. After 10 years of dispute, in 325 AD, Arianism was defeated at the first great Council at Nicaea, though not of course eliminated. The level of controversy over the way in which the divinity of Christ was to be put into words rose and fell as church and imperial politics became intertwined over the following centuries. But it was all a very long time ago! The meanings of Greek and Latin words translated as 'essence', 'nature' or 'substance' with their Aristotelian underpinning, are effectively lost to us now. Every generation still has the arguments. David Jenkins (later Bishop of Durham), when a tutor at Oxford, once commented that all the questions which need to be asked about the divinity of Jesus were asked in those first centuries – but that none of those answers work now!

So how does John help us understand how God was present in Jesus? Was Jesus uniquely similar to or uniquely identical with God? That he was unique no one doubted. John often uses the verb 'send' to describe what God has done. This might seem to favour the former interpretation and we can find more 'distancing' language in the extended section in Chapter 5 (5 vv19–24). But then John is at pains to affirm that Jesus' enemies thought that by claiming to be 'sent' he 'was calling God his own Father thereby making himself equal with God' (5 v18). In a later exchange Jesus himself provokes a possible stoning for blasphemy by actually claiming 'before Abraham was, I am' (8 v58). We must face the fact that no human language, whether Greek or Latin, English or even German, can describe God! Better to settle for the two matching affirmations of faith in what has been revealed: God chose Jesus and God chose to be Jesus. John is at pains to affirm both the human and the divine natures, though unlike Paul he nowhere uses the word 'nature'. Our verse uses the verb 'gave' but that, too, is not intended to distance God from the Son. Like all the New Testament writers, John recognises that Jesus' followers came to realise, some sooner than others, that this man they had been following, in whom they trusted, was somehow the unique embodiment of God's loving nature lived out among them. This meant that death could not hold him and, crucially, that his death and resurrection therefore was truly an act of God.

Then take the word 'may'. This is not 'will', which would point far ahead, promising life beyond death. In terms of the 'when' of salvation there is again a contrast with the Synoptics. There Jesus' teaching mostly contrasts the here and now with a kingdom beyond this world, a kingdom of heaven starkly contrasted with earth. Heaven is where God's will is done (as in the Lord's Prayer) or associated with the future coming of a bridegroom or a thief in the night. But for John eternal life is a transformation of the here and now. The 'final' judgement is not deferred beyond death, as in Greek mythology and many other religious traditions. Rather, as John Marsh puts it: 'the real situation is not that the world will go on and at the end the judgement will come, but rather that because God has acted from his universal love and offered to all the gift of life freely, judgement takes place within history, now'.[41] This is also implicit in the theology of Paul but he prefers, as usual, the metaphorical language of the courtroom: 'justification' has been achieved through the death of Jesus so that 'there is therefore now no condemnation for those who are in Christ Jesus' (Romans 8 v1). Similarly, the thrust of John's verse is that our response to Jesus Christ is the final judgement. For him there is no courtroom language, with overtones of guilt and acquittal, but the more familiar setting of daily discernment of what can be done by a disciple in faith and love. He continues in this passage with a stark contrast between light and darkness: 'And this is the judgement, that the light has come into the world and people loved darkness rather than light ...' (3 vv19ff). No nuanced shades of 'maybe' for John the preacher. He concludes: 'those who do the truth come to the light, so that it may be clearly seen that their deeds have been done in God' (3 v21).

The climatic passage at the close of Chapter 12 before John launches into the Passion narrative unpacks this single condensed verse, 3 v16. It focuses on the interpretation of the 'now' which some have called 'realised' eschatology, meaning that the present time is the final (the ultimate) judgement anticipated. In the words of T. S. Eliot, 'Time present and time past/are both perhaps present in time future/and time future contained in time past' (Burnt Norton). Thus we read: 'Then Jesus cried aloud: "Whoever believes in me believes not in me but in him who sent me. And whoever sees me sees him who sent me ... I do not judge anyone who hears my words and does not keep them, for I came not to judge the world, but to save the world. The one who rejects me and does not receive my word has a judge; on the last day the word that I have spoken will serve as judge"' (12 vv44ff). No one must perish but those who so choose may.

And lastly, what of the actual word 'perish' in this rich verse. Are we listening for echoes of the wild Book of Revelation, another book by another John? That those who do not accept what God is doing in Jesus, who do not believe, are condemned is spelt out. But condemned to what? Within the context of this verse the contrast is clearly with 'eternal life'. The word translated as 'perish' or 'be lost' comes from the Greek word meaning 'be destroyed'. And what is the opposite of life but death? But in John's Gospel there are none of the more apocalyptic visions of the Synoptics, the torment endured by the rich man who ignored the beggar (Luke 16 vv19ff) or the 'eternal fire prepared for the devil and his angels' (Matthew 25 v41). When Judas leaves the company intent on his devilish betrayal, 'and it was night' is all that John says. He offers almost an understatement: 'on the last day the word that I have spoken will serve as judge' (12 v48). John is intent on emphasising the positive, the opportunity, the offer of life through faith in Jesus as Christ. He does not seek to frighten anyone into faith like some 'hell-fire' preacher. One is almost reminded of the death of Socrates who speculates that either there will be life beyond death with so many great and interesting people to meet, or there will be nothing; to the last that great agnostic does not know what to believe from two unproven hypotheses. That cross-reference is of course unfair! But John offers the simple word 'perish' as the default destiny which he sets against the abundant life so full of God's love that it will not be ended by death. Unbelievers will miss out on the continuing love of God beyond time. The promise is so wonderful that he does not need to scare his readers into faith but rather invites them to believe and to live the life of God now and for ever.

Chapter 9

The Word and the Words

There is an irony in the fact that *'Search the Scriptures'* is the title of a Bible Study series published through the Inter-Varsity Press, a conservative evangelical body which holds to a fairly literalist view of the authority of the Bible. Ironical because of the original context of this quote in John 5 v30: 'You search the scriptures because you think that in them you have eternal life; and it is they that testify on my behalf. Yet you refuse to come to me to have life.' The authority of scripture is rendered somewhat secondary by Jesus when it is used by his interlocutors to evade or resist the demands of a living faith!

One of the main themes of all four Gospels is that Jesus fulfilled the promises of the scriptures. All the New Testament writers are at pains to claim and explain that the Christian message is the direct outcome of the scriptures (our Old Testament). Several times in John as in the Synoptics it is spelt out, 'as it is written' or 'this was to fulfil what was spoken by the prophet', with a relevant reference.

Jesus is pictured as going to the heart of the biblical message; John echoes Mark 1 v22, 'he taught as one having authority and not as the scribes'. But there is a paradox here: those who claimed to understand the scriptures best were those who could not cope with Jesus. There is another related strand running through the Gospels: that Jesus is indeed the Messiah but not the one that almost everyone was expecting from their reading of scripture. There had been a number of claimants, including a certain Judas whose Galilean rebellion around 7 AD might have been witnessed by Jesus as a child, along with the mass crucifixion of his followers. Doubtless such rebellions took their inspiration from the scriptural promises of restoration and supremacy and election. These are, after all, more frequent than the prophecies such as those in the book of Isaiah which call on Israel to be the Servant of the Lord, even a suffering servant.[42] It is not hard to see how, from the pages of the Hebrew Scriptures (especially the inter-testamental writings about the Maccabean revolts), the popular expectation of a strong leader, almost certainly a military campaigner would take hold. He would arrive as the Lord's 'Anointed' (which is what 'Messiah' means) and re-establish God's kingdom like a second David.

Jesus consciously seeks to fulfil the scriptures by a radical re-interpretation. By going back to basics he suffered what all would-be reformers have suffered, when his call to 'repent and believe in the good news' (Mark 1 v15) is resisted. In a similar vein one might say Martin Luther first tried to introduce reform within the Catholic Church and John Wesley within the Church of England; both after some years were forced into schism. Some commentators claim that Luke implies that even on Palm Sunday Jesus hoped against hope that his mission would result in a spiritual revival. This would re-establish God's People as such, the outcome which he and John the Baptist had set out to achieve. But resistance to change prevailed.

The first Christians had to scour their scriptures to find passages and texts which might validate their understanding of Jesus as the Christ. There is no doubt that Jesus himself had done this thoroughly too, of course, even if they did not understand his interpretations until after the Resurrection. 'We thought he was the one' (meaning the Messiah) say the sad disciples trudging home after the death of their hero (Luke 24 v21). The stranger who joined them on that road replies with an exposition in which 'beginning with Moses and all the prophets, he interpreted to them the things about himself in all the scriptures' (Luke 24 v27). What a Bible study! That 'interpretation' was a central task of the new church. Paul, writing to the church in Corinth around 55 AD, was reflecting a general understanding in the Church when he asserts that Christ died for our sins and that he was raised on the third day, both 'in accordance with the scriptures' (I Corinthians 15 vv1ff). In fact this simple phrase is debatable and its allusions to actual passages is unclear. All four gospel writers elaborated or even re-wrote episodes in the life of Jesus to fit more closely with a prophecy from scripture; such was their desire for 'biblical' authority.

There is a deceptively wise saying, that the Bible says things because they are true – they are not true because they are in the Bible. The authority of scripture has always been ambivalent. 'You can prove anything from the Bible' is a familiar cliché (depending on what you might mean by 'prove'). And from the Qur'an, too, but that's another story. Jesus' frustration with the scholars in John 5 v30 is repeated through the Gospel and through the centuries. What is it about the concept of Holy Scripture which gives it power? Our New Testament is, after all, the selection of books in which Christians discerned the Word of God. There were several other texts which the Church declined to include in their selection of Christian scripture. Discovery of the manuscripts of some of these lost books has generated much speculation about the process of agreeing on what became an agreed canon of a New Testament. The paradox is that we are a People of the Book which is at the same time the book of the people! In its foundation statements the United Reformed Church attempts to balance the paradox thus: 'the Word of God in the Old and New Testaments, discerned under the guidance of the Holy Spirit, (is) the supreme authority for all God's people'. Without discernment the Word cannot be heard, still less obeyed. Charles Wesley puts it thus:

Still we believe, almighty Lord,
whose presence fills both earth and heaven,
the meaning of the written word
is by thy inspiration given;

thou only dost thyself explain,
the secret mind of God make plain.[43]

But as Sydney Carter sang:

The living truth is what I long to see;
I cannot lean upon what used to be.
So shut your Bible up and show me how
the Christ you talk about is living now.[44]

We do need to confront the elusive concept of biblical authority head on. From the very first and in every generation, Christians have been busily engaged in a trawl through the Bible, initially the Hebrew Scriptures, to gain authority for their positions or statements or whatever. Today, believers and unbelievers alike are often found labouring under a serious misapprehension in the use of biblical quotations. For example, several militant atheists appear to think that the stories of an apparently blood-thirsty God in, say, the book of Joshua discredit religious faith as such, including Christianity. But 'that God you don't believe in, I don't believe in either!' (ascribed to Reb Levi Yitzhak around 1800). Between Christians, too, many disagreements about morality and behaviour appear to end up in arguments about the Bible. John is no different in wanting to claim that Jesus is fulfilling the promises and prophecies of scripture – but in this passage (5 vv19ff) he has to acknowledge that no one can simply read off what God is saying for all time irrespective of context.

The very phrase 'proof text' gives the game away: no one starts with their scriptures – they are being used to prove something. It is important to realise that all Christians, from the avowedly literalist through to the most liberal, are actually using the phrase 'Word of God' to refer to an authoritative *interpretation* of the Bible rather than to the text on its own. It is faith in God and in Christ (kindled by a range of stimuli, including of course the Bible) that colours the interpretation of scripture and not the other way round. For all interpreters and debaters the question (whether spoken or unspoken) 'who is Christ?' or even 'what is right?' comes well ahead of 'what does the Bible say?'. We all do this, whether conservative or liberal. We do not actually start with the Bible. Some of us were brought up on the 'Scofield Reference Bible', a heavily annotated edition of the King James Version which purported to transform the scriptures into an instant '*summa*' of incontrovertible dogma.[45] But thank God one can discover (mainly by reading it!) that the Bible is not that kind of book. It is a library of 66 books, with at least as many writers, including narrative, poetry, anecdote, correspondence, speculation, preaching, legend, 'spin' and prophecy. Everyone knows that you can find disagreements or inconsistencies between the writers of the Bible. Yet in debate after debate people come to a view and then look for 'suitable' passages; we all do this. Even compilers of lectionaries acknowledge this, omitting passages which might be misunderstood or lead the faithful astray! This helps to explain why the proponents of different approaches or stances will appeal to different biblical passages, notoriously on a contentious issue like homosexuality. One side quote a handful of verses out of context as though they were trumping their opponents' high cards; the other side may do the same. But in this argument as in so many others, scripture is being used as a secondary authority to back up a position already adopted on other grounds and these grounds are overwhelmingly cultural and contextual.

The wise theologian and philosopher Leonard Hodgson describes the authentic sequence of biblical interpretation, beginning with checking on textual accuracy, heading through what the author meant or intended, but always arriving at the vital question 'what must the truth have been if it appeared like this to people who thought like that?'.[46] (There is an example of this sequence in the following chapter.) Biblical interpretation, like church life generally, has always reflected the contemporary *zeitgeist*, the mood of society as a whole, whether authoritarian or sceptical, obedient or rebellious, cautious or permissive, exclusive or inclusive. John Campbell pictures this very well in his 'Being Biblical' and uses this quote from Albert Schweitzer: 'each successive epoch of theology found its own thoughts in Jesus ... and each individual created him in accordance with his own character'.[47] This is how it has always been, not least in Jesus' own time as John demonstrates in this passage. There is nothing untoward or perverse with that, always provided it is acknowledged, which sadly is only rarely, such is the hankering after biblical authority.

Thus, as we learn from such episodes, if authority (God's will) equals tradition, you may get one interpretation of scripture; but if authority equals sensitivity to change you may get a different one. This is as true today as it was when Jesus almost lost his cool in the face of the biblical literalists of his day. The passage from 5 vv39–47 is very dense, but the challenge of Jesus to his accusers is that 'if you believed Moses, you would believe me, for he wrote about me', which is serious enough. Then he concludes 'but if you do not believe what he wrote, how then will you believe what I say?' which is even more devastating. From Nicodemus in Chapter 3 to Caiaphas in Chapter 11, Jesus is on a collision course with those literalists who will not accept that the Word might be alive, God still speaking as the creative, saving and life-giving Spirit free as the wind (3 vv6ff). To re-work Sydney Carter's rather desperate plea, we need to *open up* the Bible and 'show me how the Christ you talk about is living now'. That is the calling of those who honour the Word beyond the words in the spirit of John's Gospel.

For Christians it is vital to realise that the collection of books which comprise the New Testament are themselves interpretations, inspired and splendidly diverse. Inevitably the writers have each approached the subject to express their own faith and experience, their own understanding of the message of Jesus and the message about Jesus as Christ and Lord. Of course their own personalities coloured their presentations and their selection of material. As we saw, John is not the only Gospel-writer to tweak his narrative to suit his theology; they all did it. A poor analogy might be that of considering Government (any Government) which from a distance seems a single power but which, the closer you get, is actually a cluster of different and rival Departments, sometimes in conflict and always in competition, and yet somehow a unified authority. There is a valuable and creative diversity in the different approaches of the New Testament writers. This is why a focus on a single writer, such as John in this book, is itself bound to result in an incomplete picture. Behind the texts there is a roomful of inspired witnesses whose cumulative testimony persuaded the church over the centuries to set their writings on a par with the Hebrew Scriptures (a much more diverse collection!) for use in worship, evangelism and teaching. The trick is to listen to what they say and then, as Rowan Williams puts it: 'be ... listeners, quiet enough to learn how to tune in to what God wants us to hear in the words of the Bible'.[48] It may be something new!

Chapter 10

'Has No One Condemned You?'

In the previous chapter we noted that the theologian and philosopher Leonard Hodgson describes the authentic sequence of biblical interpretation, beginning with checking on textual accuracy or probability, heading through what the author meant or intended, but always arriving at the vital question 'what must the truth have been if it appeared like this to people who thought like that?' Each stage of this careful process is relevant when we look at a passage usually placed at the start of John Chapter 8, the story of the woman taken in adultery.

Unlike Chapter 21, which may possibly be from a different hand but appears in all the manuscripts, these verses are missing from all but one of the Greek manuscripts. They first appear in the earliest Latin translations, including Jerome's in the late fourth century which was later known as the 'Vulgate', meaning 'of the people' because it was so widely used. The popularity of that version meant that the passage was eventually included in the translation finalised in 1611, sponsored by King James, and known as the 'Authorised Version'. This became the definitive English text for over three centuries. The passage appears in the *codex bezae*, a manuscript from the fifth century which includes a Latin version alongside the Greek. That manuscript was being used by translators and interpreters in the centuries before earlier manuscripts were unearthed. All this textual history suggests that this is a passage which circulated in the Latin-speaking church and that other copiers, if they knew of it, did not include it. Indeed, some older manuscripts even have a special mark at the end of Chapter 7, indicating a possible deliberate omission. So there may be some truth in the wry comment from Augustine, again around 400 AD, which suspects modesty – or worse – on the part of copiers: 'Certain persons of little faith, or rather enemies of the true faith, fearing, I suppose, lest their wives should be given impunity in sinning, removed from their manuscripts the Lord's act of forgiveness toward the adulteress, as if he who had said "Sin no more" had granted permission to sin.'[49] Had punctuation been developed at the time, Augustine might well have concluded with a large exclamation mark.

Commentators also note the variations of style and of vocabulary in this passage as compared with the rest of the gospel. The fact that there are so many variant readings of this passage (as compared with the rest of the gospel) also points to a reasonable conclusion that it was not there in the original. But it does come a few verses before Jesus, in continuing confrontation with the Jewish leaders, remarks, 'You judge by human standards; I judge no one' (8 v15), which may well explain why it was inserted at that point. Interestingly, one manuscript from the late Middle Ages inserts the story into Luke's Gospel.[50] This is clearly theologically driven, in that one can readily imagine the Jesus portrayed by Luke as acting in this way. In summary it appears to be an authentic story, one of a large number which were circulating alongside those which were eventually chosen for their records by our four gospel writers. Though probably not in John's Gospel originally, those who included it recognised that it does develop his teaching about love and judgement and the need to trust Jesus as Saviour.

The incident is one of several encounters with Jewish leaders where they try to trap Jesus into saying something which may be used in evidence against him. As with the question about paying tribute to Caesar, Jesus has the choice between denying the authority of Rome or that of Moses. If he agrees that the woman should be stoned, he might be charged with challenging the Roman system of justice by acting as a magistrate; whereas if he disagrees, he is going against the Law of Moses (Deuteronomy

22 vv23f). As with the question about paying tax to Caesar (Mark 12 vv13ff) Jesus finesses the question and sidesteps the trap. Some commentators interpret his writing in the sand as a parallel to the practice of a Roman magistrate writing out the verdict before delivering it; or maybe Jesus was letting the noise die down, for it would have been an angry lynch mob. There is a touch of psychological drama when the accusers slink away, 'beginning with the eldest', for it was the role of Elders to initiate the stoning so their unwillingness triggers the failure of nerve on the part of the whole crowd. Jesus, maybe alone with the woman by then, refuses to condemn and sends her away to 'sin no more'.

But we do need to move on to Hodgson's main question ('what must the truth have been if it appeared like this to people who thought like that?'). For this we are taken back to John 3 17: God's love for the world overrides what the more legalist theologians would regard as justice: 'God did not send the Son into the world to condemn the world but that the world might be saved through him.' Those familiar with the pattern of Hebrew writing would appreciate this as a repetition (known as parallelism) of what has already been said in the previous verse. There we read: 'God so loved the world that he gave his only Son so that everyone who believes in him may not perish but have eternal life.' In this stylistic device the next verse or phrase repeats, from a different perspective, what has just been stated, by way of reinforcement rather than as a development of the idea or statement. So we may take the pair of verses together as a consolidated affirmation and conclude that salvation for John is the outcome of trust in God's non-condemnatory love. The evangelist's claim is that this belief leads to life, the same claim which John makes in summarising his message '... these things are written that you may believe ... and through believing you may have life in his name' (20 v31). 'Saved' in 3 v17 is a rare word for John, more familiar in Paul's writing.[51] As we have seen,

John's view of faith and its outcome is more about the triumph of love over hate (as in this little story), light over darkness and life over death.

Throughout John's Gospel the initiative of God in love overrides what humankind might otherwise deserve. The implications of this are worked out in greater depth in the 'upper room discourses' about love; but divine love is the dominant note throughout the book. In short, it is self-giving, compassionate, unbounded love which is the life of God demonstrated in the incarnate Word. A youth leader friend of mine once mischievously summed up what so many people experience of the church: 'In the beginning was the word – and the word was "no!".' For John the Word was emphatically 'Yes!'. This little story, perhaps too 'liberal' for the early copiers, shows just how inclusive was this love for the world and for this particular woman. 'Whoever comes to me I will not turn away' (6 v37) is still a problem for some of Christ's followers, would-be gatekeepers who wish to define the boundaries and set limits on the love of this God.

Jesus does not condone her sin but he does release her. We are not even told whether she repented her undeniable sin before being forgiven. Other theologies would require confession and penitence before forgiveness, before grace can abound. Not so here. As in other episodes, people can say 'no' to Jesus and to the Father who sent him. But for those who say 'yes' there is life and love: 'I give them eternal life and they will never perish; no one will snatch them out of my hand' (10 v28). This 'fallen woman' is one of many who are rescued by such a good shepherd.

Chapter 11

New Life for Old

Moving on, there is another lengthy episode which rarely gets read in full in church, the raising of Lazarus (11, vv1–44). This again is a 'sign', a representative story. Missing from this chapter is any personal characterisation as found in the earlier encounters with the anonymous Samaritan woman or the blind man. Though Lazarus was special ('see how he loved him!' 11 v36) and someone whose notoriety put him in danger from the authorities (12 v10), John gives us no personal portrait. Rather the narrative is totally focused on the deeper and wider issues, though it does contain the celebrated shortest verse in the Bible, beloved of quiz-setters, 'Jesus wept' (11 v35) in response to Mary's tears. Much as Yahweh, the Lord, intervenes first in history when he sees the plight of the Hebrews in Egypt, so Jesus embodies an essentially compassionate God who 'loved the world so much' and has now acted to rescue humankind. Lazarus stands for those who are in Paul's words 'dead in their sins', and then set free from the power of sin and death.

But if Lazarus is not described as an individual, his sisters Martha and Mary do come across as the same characters we meet in Luke 10. Martha represents believers who will say the creeds, do their duty, keep the show on the road, puzzled and even a little resentful when life does not go according to plan; she is the practical one who protests at the re-opening of a tomb after four days. Mary represents those whose love of God overflows sometimes irrationally, for whom one relationship is worth ten propositions, whose prayers are from the heart and certainly not just from the book. They both reproach Jesus, 'if you had been here, my brother would not have died' (11 vv21, 32) but his responses are as different as the two of them. Martha needs some doctrinal assurance, Mary needs some personal comfort. John's readers include both.

It is often said that Lazarus rises 'merely' to physical life. But as with the man born blind there is an inner renewal, a new kind of life, which John covets for his readers. From the outset Jesus has made this clear. In Mark (2 v5) he says to the paralysed man brought by his friends for healing 'your sins are forgiven'; the subsequent physical healing is but a signal of a far more important restoration of well-being. This climactic miraculous raising of Lazarus is similarly for John a sign, a representative and symbolic act of the Word made flesh. For John and for all believers the resurrection of Jesus himself 'is not a conjuring trick with bones', as Bishop David Jenkins said (as opposed to what he was reported as saying!).[52] It is new life, God's eternal life on earth as it is in heaven, 'life in all its fulness' (10 v10), offered to all, here and now and forever. Even so, it is a promise often misunderstood.

There is little doubt that it was this promise of eternal or everlasting life which formed the heart of Christian preaching as the apostles took their message around the Mediterranean and beyond. Over the centuries the notion of life after death has been mocked and misused, distorted and deconstructed, by believers and by opponents. If one asks what John means, commentators usually start with the context of contemporary beliefs and ideas. First there was the widespread belief, common to very many traditions, that things must surely be put right 'somewhere', after death. Justice implies a 'somewhere' and probably a 'someone', given the unfairness of much human experience. Traditional Greek and Roman religion included such beliefs about an afterlife. At that time there were, as we saw, several 'mystery religions' promising a spiritual life, otherworldly and escapist, of a distinctly esoteric and fantastic sort. These cults were the basis of the later Christian deviation into Gnosticism. Again, there will have been some believers in reincarnation, hinted at by some Greek philosophers and imported by devotees of Asian religions. And then there were the Jews, or at least some of them, who in the previous century or so had come to realise that resurrection was the logical conclusion of their faith. The Pharisees held this belief, which the Sadducees rejected. Jesus was clear that when God said to Moses, 'I am the God of Abraham, the God of Isaac and the God of Jacob' it was evident that 'He is God not of the dead but of the living' (Mark 12 vv26f). We might want to add alternative meanings from closer to our own times, such as those who believe that creative artists, including composers, writers, painters, etc., live on in their work. And most recently there are plenty of people who recognise the continuing 'presence' of those who have died in the traits or genetic make-up of subsequent generations.

But for John none of these points are relevant because his exclusive focus is on Jesus as Christ. The promise of eternal life was part and parcel of the core belief in the incarnation and its inevitable consequences, the resurrection and giving of the Holy Spirit. Not that it would have occurred to John, or any of the disciples or other New Testament writers, to consider that Jesus might not have been a human being, mortal like us. Believers do not say of the resurrection 'well, he was God so what do you expect?'. But as they reflected on the total phenomenon of Jesus, John and the others came to acknowledge that God had been uniquely present with them in him and that therefore God's love and God's life were one. Thus Paul can write: 'The life I now live is not my life but the life which Christ lives in me' (Galatians 2 v20). For John Jesus not only taught this but embodied it, equating the life and the love of God. And where the latter is, there is the former, a kind of living like Jesus (albeit imperfectly) through the Spirit. John preached not that eternal life was some kind of reward beyond death, but that God's life of love can be lived here in part and hereafter in full. This is the thrust of John's message and the key to its appeal back then and through the centuries.

With the story of the raising of Lazarus John brings his sequence of significant episodes and interviews to a close, finally rising above metaphor, for life is not really a metaphor like water or light. The celebratory dinner which Jesus attends (12 vv1ff) on the evening before the final entry into Jerusalem is held in the context of rising tension; the authorities have already issued a warrant for his arrest (11 v57). With the raising of Lazarus the ministry of Jesus is fulfilled; now all that remains is for God to authenticate it on the cross and in the Easter garden.

Chapter 12

The High Priest

Caiaphas is, for John, the key person among those who contrived to get Jesus killed. You will not find his name as High Priest in Mark's Gospel at all; Matthew and Luke give his name only *en passant*, as it were, as for them his father-in-law Annas was still pulling the strings in the Sanhedrin. It is in John that we find Caiaphas as a character in the drama. This is not too surprising, since the Fourth Gospel, with its Jerusalem memories, offers the most credible version of the actual events of those few days, a tangled story of intrigue and mixed motives of which John le Carré might be proud.

If we consider the verses from John Chapter 11 in which Caiaphas makes his famous statement, the background is the raising of Lazarus of Bethany from the dead. The Bethany home of Lazarus and his sisters, Mary and Martha, was where Jesus stayed when he was in the Jerusalem area, a few miles out of town. Even without any media coverage, the crowds soon learned of this miracle and went to gawp at Lazarus. Many of them became convinced by what they saw, that Jesus must be the promised Messiah.

John writes (11 vv45ff) that this popularity sent shock-waves through the Jerusalem establishment. The Sanhedrin was summoned, maybe to a special meeting, and debated what to do. Caiaphas laid out the political stakes very clearly: 'You know nothing at all! You do not understand that it is better for you to have one man die for the people than to have the whole nation destroyed.' Trouble would mean the Romans replacing their relatively light-touch authority with a more harsh and oppressive regime or even worse. The current arrangement (very tolerant of local customs and religion compared with some other occupied territories) was a delicate balance.

As to the dramatic flow, this was a preliminary meeting of the kind familiar in all organisations (including religious ones), a caucus where the real decision is made. The arrest and show trial, with its agreed verdict, would follow a little later. The fact that the timing went wrong and the deal made with Pilate nearly came unstuck will be no surprise to anyone familiar with attempts at conspiracy.

There is also the financial interest, of course. As High Priest Caiaphas was joint head of the Sadducees, probably known to other traders as *cosa nostra*! They held the monopoly of the currency exchange and the pilgrim or tourist trade at the Temple, a massive earner at Festival time with several thousand people turning up and needing to pay the Temple tax in the special currency and buy their animals for sacrifices. They had indeed made it a den of robbers. Jesus embodied a profound threat to their livelihood as well as their status.

John is not a journalist, however, not even an investigative one. Maybe the gist of the meeting reached him via Nicodemus or another sympathiser. The thrust of his account is to affirm a deeper truth, even if that truth is spoken unwittingly, as here. What a High Priest said by way of official pronouncement had come to be deemed a word from the Lord, *'ex cathedra'* one might say. Even when the office is held unworthily, this authority might still apply to what was said. John takes a delight in pointing out that Caiaphas' statement was genuine prophecy, but in a totally opposite way from what was intended. Truly Jesus does 'die for the people'. It is John's purpose here to show how human motives and reasoning are overruled by the divine plan unfolding. The status under God of Temple and nationhood are to be redefined and if necessary bypassed if the religious leaders reject Jesus as God's Messiah. John has another reason to highlight the role of Caiaphas as High Priest. Once a year on Yom Kippur, the Day of Atonement, the High Priest was allowed to enter the innermost sanctuary in the Temple, the Holy of Holies. There he offered sacrifices on behalf of the whole nation. In that year, and John is at pains to mention 'in that year' three times (though he and Annas were High Priests for almost 20 years), Caiaphas offered up Jesus, whom we know – because John has told us – is the Lamb of God who takes away the sin of the world. Though the High Priest's sacrifice is not a lamb the imagery is nevertheless breathtaking.

Caiaphas interests John in what he stands for. And why should we bother with Caiaphas today? We need to be careful. There are contemporary arguments around the behaviour of Israel as a nation-state. That was the issue nearest to Caiaphas' heart. It's a live enough issue for us too. But it's not what mattered to John.

It is also tempting to develop the theme of religious dissent, the failure of Caiaphas and his party to draw any serious conscientious lines in dealings with the Romans. We could remind ourselves of all those, including those in our own time, who have discovered their sticking point when Caesar starts playing at God and when some of God's representatives allow them to get away with it. There are many witnesses (in Greek 'martyrs') who have resisted such false claims to the death and we are right to honour and marvel at them, from that first century to our own time.

But the significance of Caiaphas for John is what his part in the story tells us about Jesus. That is, after all, John's purpose in writing his book, to persuade us that Jesus is God's initiative, the embodiment of God's love.

So the key aspect of the representative figure of the High Priest Caiaphas for John is the challenge which, albeit in love and humility, Christianity offers to Judaism. This has been one of John's principal themes throughout his book. Whenever we describe Jesus as Christ we are calling him Messiah. Caiaphas simply could not see Jesus as that figure; Christians have always affirmed that this is who he is. By far the largest part of the recorded preaching and teaching of the New Testament turns on this question. Paul's preaching is grounded on the belief that Jesus is the Christ; that was the truth which struck him on the Damascus road. It was at the core of his message whenever he arrived at a fresh town and started to preach, usually in the local synagogue. The time has come, God has acted, this is the good news which will save you. Try reading Paul's letters and replacing the word Christ with Messiah and see what a page of Paul's writing feels like. Then imagine you're Caiaphas reading it!

Relationships between Christians and Jews over the centuries have been rarely as cordial as today, by and large; sometimes they have been poisonous or downright wretched. Even now at one extreme are those who believe that the 'new covenant' has completely replaced the old, such that Jews as such are no more God's chosen people; John does tend towards this view. At the other extreme are some who will blur all distinctions of faith and welcome anyone with a spiritual or religious practice as brothers and sisters. Somewhere on this spectrum we find contemporary conversations. All inter-faith dialogue is awkward and asymmetrical, however friendly on a personal level; its goal is unclear but its by-products are often very valuable. Relations between Christians and Jews need more attention than other bilateral contacts, not least because of the evil treatment of European Jews under the Nazi regime and the subsequent foundation of the state of Israel. Today the word 'Israel' has at least five meanings: the historical biblical state founded by Moses and Joshua, the later post-Solomon state ('the northern kingdom') with a capital in Samaria, the spiritual sense of being God's chosen people, the contemporary almost secular state of Israel, and the metaphor often used by Christians to describe themselves as 'chosen' in hymns and dramas. These meanings are easily blurred. Certainly criticism of the fourth of those is often perceived as criticism of the third, and any anti-Zionism decried as anti-Semitism.[53] As in Jesus' time contemporary Israeli political groups can manoeuvre to their secular advantage from behind the claim of being special, 'God's chosen people'. But anti-Semitism is, among other things, a denial of the promises in the Hebrew Scriptures and thus a very complex matter for followers of Jesus Christ.

Throughout John's Gospel there is the deep spiritual challenge: what actually is faith? Caiaphas is not alone in finding it impossible to believe in a living God, whose promises are not for ever deferred, whose time might very well be the present, not only the distant past or future. We saw the same in the meeting with Nicodemus in Chapter 3. But imagine you are Caiaphas for a moment. You receive reports of a dynamic young preacher challenging his hearers that 'whoever would save his life must lose it' (12 v25). You are not stupid; you understand full well that it's you he's talking about, your sacred office, your God-given institutions, your religious practice, your social position, your power, your wealth, your reputation, even your life. Laying down all that is not for Caiaphas and his like in any situation!

Was it possible for Caiaphas to do and say other than he did? Probably not. Do we have to rehabilitate him? Again, probably not. He represents a tendency in all leaders, certainly including religious leaders, to circle the wagons when criticism arises, to identify a scapegoat, to misrepresent and 'spin' against their critics, to mis-time their confrontations and as often as not to end up in a worse place! It is a sadly familiar pattern of institutional behaviour which is almost universal across all cultures and in every century, certainly in every Christian denomination in our own times. Although for John, Caiaphas is only a walk-on part, he is worth our attention when we too are tempted to resist the free wind blowing, the spirit of a living God. Those who are tempted to play the gatekeeper are at risk of exclusion themselves.

Chapter 13

Judas and Mary

Just what are we to make of the encounter between Judas and Mary and Jesus' reported rebuke of Judas (12 vv1–8)? Most commentaries focus on the comparison of this story with those in Mark (14 vv3–9) and Luke (7 vv36ff) but these few verses in John are more about a perennial ethical dilemma for all religions and their devoted adherents. In the Synoptics we do not have Jesus' strange saying 'you will always have the poor with you but you do not always have me', though it is implied in Matthew's passage where Jesus identifies with 'the least of these' (Matthew 25 v40).

For a start, we can discount any suggestion that Jesus, of all people, meant 'poverty is a never-ending fact of history so it will be a waste of time and effort trying to eradicate it'. He certainly does not mean that believers can leave social welfare to others and stick to private religion. But there is certainly a case to answer if 'private religion' is perceived as damaging 'social welfare'. Unfortunately, in a Christian text, the role of Judas does distort any analysis. Judas was absolute anathema to the first Christians, i.e. he is bound to be in the wrong here. Nearly every mention of him in the New Testament and beyond carries the tag-line 'the one who turned traitor' or words to that effect. But we have to listen to his challenge to Mary even if we do not need to rehabilitate him in order to do so. The fact remains that what Judas said is being repeated with increasing force as the scale of world poverty and division becomes apparent to anyone with a television. Remembering that, both economically and psychologically, the opposite of 'poverty' is not 'riches' but 'inclusion' or 'fairness', it becomes evident that the prospects for the poor are bleak as inequality, within nations and across the globe, intensifies.

'Why was this perfume not sold for 300 denarii and the money given to the poor?' (12 v5). Today's critic knows that we do not have the physical body of Jesus on which to lavish our love. He who was dead and embalmed is risen and ascended and, in that crude sense, unavailable for anointing. But did not Jesus make the poor his heirs? Are not Judas' words a rebuke of Church practice over the centuries, the priorities of extravagantly funded buildings, stained glass memorials, chantries, vestments, tapestries, organs and the rest? Are we not bound to show any extravagant impulses we might have towards the poor rather than splash out on such things, or must they forever watch us like the beggar watched the rich man in Luke 16? And this contemporary Judas, with a keen eye for hypocrisy, can see that an undeniably high proportion of the money spent on church building and decoration is in great measure a matter of prestige or self-indulgence. Mighty cathedrals and churches in all traditions are built and endowed *Ad Maiorem Dei Gloriam* ('to the greater glory of God') which may be the motto of the humble Jesuits but is a frequent disguise for extraordinary self-publicity on the part of patrons, be they mediaeval monarchs or nineteenth-century successful businessmen, all looking out for their reputational legacy.

Such critics do have a case even if, of course, they exaggerate. Often this critical voice is a cover for their attack on the church as such: we are deceiving ourselves (as believers) in perpetuating the irrelevancies of religion and the mythologies of God when we should be devoting ourselves to addressing the needs of the world's peoples. 'Christian Aid' ought to represent 90 per cent of the church's outgoings if not 100 per cent. And in response, the church and its leadership do often sound like failed business leaders defending established practices. Thus if our ancestors gave this beautiful church (probably a listed building!) it is down to us to protect and refurbish it for their sakes, rather than turn a capital asset into a relief fund.

So where might extravagance feature in Christian practice? The issue is how to discern authentic gratitude, says John. In Mark, followed by Luke but not Matthew, we find a similar story of Jesus commending a poor widow who put a precious two mites into the Temple treasury. That gift meant more in Jesus' eyes than the largesse of those who could easily afford what they gave. By the laws of domestic economics she was as wasteful as Mary with the perfume. Jesus knew that her money as money counted for little; but, in an irresistible cliché, it's the thought that counts. William Temple reflects on the story in John: 'To the worldly mind such acts of devotion are always foolish; yet it is true that where lavish expenditure expresses the over-flowing of a heart's devotion, it is unspeakably precious.'[54] Extravagance is a mark of love – and it keeps jewellers in business. It is not the price that matters most. Economic calculation may despise such 'wasteful' impulses and simple open-heartedness. But the term 'humanity' belongs with such instincts and lifts our species above baser animal instincts for acquisition and security. In countless dramas, novels or films the heart wins over the head, tears replace frowns and *'amor vincit omnia'* (love conquers all). And what is this love but an identification with the other and the other's good, at whatever the cost? More generally it is no accident that selfishness, variously defined, is at the heart of wrong or evil in every religious tradition. The so-called 'golden rule' appears in one form or another in all moral systems, derived even indirectly from 'love your neighbour as yourself' or from 'do to others what you would have them do to you'. Unselfishness, variously defined and prescribed, is the mark of a believer and of a truly human life in almost all religious faiths, and in the higher forms of humanism too. This is never more strongly put than in John, for whom costly self-giving is the eternal nature of God himself, as revealed and demonstrated in his incarnate Son.

Matthew has recorded a challenge to a materialistic society:

'do not store up for yourselves treasures on earth, where moth and rust consume and thieves break in to steal, but store up for yourselves treasures in heaven ... for where your treasure is, there will your heart be also' (Matthew 6 v19ff). There is an authentic and necessary 'otherworldliness' in Christianity, summed up later by John: 'They do not belong to the world, just as I do not belong to the world ... As you (Father) have sent me into the world so I am sending them into the world' (17 vv16ff).

For John, the rebuke of Jesus to Judas cannot simply mean, 'when I am gone you can get on with the task of fighting poverty', just as his words to Mary cannot mean 'some day soon I will leave you to get on without me'. John's understanding of the Holy Spirit is the continuing presence of the risen Christ with his followers, so that when they live a life of costly self-giving they are indeed living out his life. Indeed, this costly, unselfish and 'unnatural' love is arguably persuasive evidence for the resurrection, even though followers of Jesus by no means have a monopoly of it.

What Judas and his fellow-critics could not and cannot appreciate is that, while the universal acknowledgement of selflessness is that it is a virtue, the heart of a distinctive Christian spirituality is a different core attitude, thankfulness. We are not searching for God but rather we are seeking to be responsive to God's search for us. Mary was thankful, and it showed. Others, albeit with often flawed motives, have felt the need to express their gratitude for God's love which is why such extravagance rings true. Gratitude may often conflict with budgetary common sense but John will not call wasteful the spontaneous offering of a generous heart in thankful response to the love of God in Christ.

Chapter 14

The Servant and the Saviour

The earliest record of Jesus' command at the Last Supper in respect of bread and wine, 'do this in remembrance of me', is found in Paul's first letter to the Christians in Corinth (11 vv23ff), then in Luke though not in Mark and Matthew who simply describe the meal. It had evidently become a tradition among Christians to fulfil this command whenever they met to share what Paul calls 'the Lord's supper' (I Corinthians 11 v20). Yet a first reading of John 13 might suggest that washing one another's feet ought to have been as sacramental as sharing bread and wine. 'If I, your Lord and Master, have washed your feet you also ought to wash one another's feet' (13 v14). A few Christian traditions have done this, but by and large the practice is confined to a few services on Maundy Thursday, most publicly those led by the Pope. In the UK it has been watered down (pardon the pun) into an eccentric act of public charity performed by the monarch with no actual washing involved at all.

So what does John think it means? Chapter 13 marks the start of the Passion narrative in John, after the 'bridge passage' of chapter 12 vv 37–50 marking the end of the public ministry and summarising the message. In Chapter 13 there is no mention of an upper room, no mention of bread and wine, no institution of the Lord's Supper or a new covenant, no mention of a Passover meal at all. As in the Synoptics, Judas is identified, indirectly, and allowed to go to fulfil his destiny. Peter is blustering in his loyalty and his triple denial is foretold. It is clearly the same event as what we call the Last Supper when we read the account in the Synoptics.

For John the episode of foot-washing sets the scene. In this action Jesus is interpreting his destiny as John understands it.

With the hindsight available to his readers, John explains the link between the death of Christ and the baptism of believers, that critical link which runs through John's portrayal of Jesus since his initial ministry alongside John the Baptist. But patiently in passage after passage since John the Baptist gave way to Jesus (3 v30) John has demonstrated that more than national renewal is now needed (the water jars of Cana are transformed in Chapter 2), the old religions are being overtaken (for Nicodemus and the Samaritan woman in Chapters 3 and 4), the power of love must trump the love of power (even for a legion of eager Galileans in Chapter 6), the Temple and its rituals are to be left behind since its custodians are like the blind leading the blind (and unwilling to be given their sight in Chapter 9). Even Lazarus' death must give way to this new life-giving presence of love, a love defined in the Greek word *agape*, echoing the divine 'loving-kindness' of Yahweh the Lord of the Hebrew Scriptures and signalling the self-sacrifice which is the true glory. It is maybe a sign that John had not read Mark's Gospel, else surely he would have quoted 'The Son of Man came not to be served but to serve' (Mark 10 v45). In similar vein, Luke has the disciples arguing even during that last supper about who should be greatest, prompting Jesus to say: 'who is greater, the one who is at the table or the one who serves? Is it not the one who sits at the table – but I am among you as one who serves' (Luke 22 v27), a parallel to John's foot-washing episode. The humility of Jesus in this symbolic act is for John a direct call to Christians to follow this example.

For Dodd the foot-washing is an authentic story, rather than a dramatisation based on words such as those quoted by Luke. He writes: 'It is far more likely that he (John) drew it independently out of tradition and then handled it after his fashion ... because the story in itself is not particularly well adapted to the purpose for which the evangelist has employed it, except insofar as the use of water for washing opens up the whole range of water-symbolism which plays so large a part in this gospel.'[55] The passage recalls the words used by Paul where he describes the double descent of Christ, first emptying himself to take the form of a slave and then 'being born in human likeness he humbled himself' (Philippians 2 vv6f). John has Jesus 'knowing ... that he had come from God and was going to God' (13 v3), then performing the foot-washing as a servant, the same pattern as in Paul.

The odd timing of Jesus' action, 'during supper' (13 v2), highlights its symbolic nature, as foot-washing was normally part of the welcome before guests sat down for the meal. Perhaps it was prompted by a conversation about personal importance such as Luke records. But it is as likely to have been a response to a change of mood on the part of Judas, whose feet Jesus also washed and for whom this action must have jarred (to say the least). As 13 v2 suggests, Jesus seems to sense a heightened tension on Judas' part, though whether Jesus was still seeking to dissuade him from carrying out his devilish intent is unlikely.

Judas is still an enigmatic figure, forever blamed as the traitor yet somehow a necessary element in the story. Much speculation as to his intentions has continued over the centuries, most recently by Amos Oz in his novel *Judas*,[56] a study in betrayal. Did he finally realise that Jesus was not the Messiah he wanted back in Galilee? Was he somehow trying to call Jesus' bluff and draw him into some act of power during the Festival or even on the cross itself? This would make his decision to leave and go to the authorities a trigger for Jesus to demonstrate that he is the Servant Messiah. Or was it just, as John also hints, a sordid story about money corrupting the banker (12 v6)? The deeper difficulty comes when Jesus says 'I am not speaking of all of you; I know whom I have chosen' (13 v18) apparently referring to Judas. Starkly put, was this a deliberate choice on Jesus' part? John finesses the question by pointing out that all the events, including the betrayal and crucifixion, are in God's plan. But centuries of debate about pre-destination and free will have not blunted the awkwardness of discussing the role of Judas. Within John's cosmic context, Judas is only the vehicle, almost an instrument, of evil. There is a paranormal ring to this: Judas is possessed and used, for John almost a 'counter-incarnation', an instrument of the real antagonist to God's purpose. For the enemy is certainly not Judas. This is a supernatural struggle. Jesus says, 'the ruler of this world is coming; but he has no power over me' (14 v30). John ignores the 'human' elements of the Judas story, the 30 pieces of silver and the kiss and the later guilty suicide. The extraordinarily poignant comment 'and it was night' (13 v30) only serves to press the unspoken and unanswerable profound question: do we blame Judas or Jesus or 'the Devil' or God? Here is the most focused and dramatic example of 'the problem of evil' since the story of Adam and Eve. Of course, for John – and his readers – this is no Socratic mealtime philosophical dialogue.[57] This is high drama in which all are caught up. Who would follow this Jesus, in that upper room or among John's first readers or now?

* * *

After Judas has left, John can proceed and Jesus can at last declare that the 'countdown' has begun: 'Now the Son of Man has been glorified and God has been glorified in him' (13 v31). The focus now turns to his own death and he continues, 'Little children, I am with you only a little longer' (13 v33), as John launches into a lengthy diversion from the narrative to spell out his (John's) deepest beliefs. Jesus is going first, his disciples will follow. As we read elsewhere: 'It was fitting that God, for whom and through whom all things exist, in bringing many children to glory, should make the pioneer of their salvation perfect through suffering' (Hebrews 2 v10). Many children are being brought to glory, the wheat is planted, the vine is to be pruned, the end is in sight. All this is God's own initiative, reinforcing the message that salvation is always a gift, the result of following Jesus. One of the few sayings that occurs almost verbatim in all four gospels makes the point: 'those who love their life in this world lose it, and those who hate their life in this world will keep it for eternal life' (12 v25). In this, Jesus is the 'pioneer of salvation' opening up a way for his followers. John adds, 'Whoever serves me must follow me; and where I am there will my servant be also' (12 v26), a sentiment repeated more than once in Chapters 14–17 as we shall see. This is salvation, life transformed in the here and now, such that death cannot destroy it because it is the life of God. The disciples may mourn but 'weeping may linger for a night but joy comes in the morning' (Psalm 30 v5). The new birth of his followers is preceded by the return (resurrection) of their Lord (16 vv20ff).

For John this supper was not a Passover meal. Jesus is killed as the Passover lambs are being killed on the following day. There is a debate over whether John deliberately altered the day of the crucifixion to fit his theology. That is possible, or he might have used an equally venerable tradition as to the date and interpreted it. Either way it is of the utmost significance for John that Jesus dies as the Lamb of God just as thousands of other lambs are being killed for the Passover feast. This does not for John mean a lamb as an offering for sin – that was not the meaning of Passover, as we will see below. It is not that John rejects a transactional, deal-making view of the cross as atonement, somehow reconciling humankind with God; he simply does not need it. His Saviour of the world is God's way, God's truth and God's life; believers need to follow the way to grasp the truth and share in the new life.

The great hymn-writer Isaac Watts (1674–1748) has written what is surely the finest poetic exposition of what John's Gospel understands by the death of Jesus:

When I survey the wondrous Cross
on which the Prince of glory died,

my richest gain I count but loss
and pour contempt on all my pride.

Forbid it, Lord, that I should boast
save in the death of Christ my God;
all the vain things that charm me most
I sacrifice them to his blood.

See from his head, his hands, his feet,
sorrow and love flow mingled down;
did e'er such love and sorrow meet,
or thorns compose so rich a crown?

His dying crimson, like a robe,
spreads o'er his body on the tree;
then I am dead to all the globe
and all the globe is dead to me.

Were the whole realm of nature mine
that were a present far too small.
Love so amazing, so divine,
demands my soul, my life, my all.

* * *

Postscript: Lamb of God

The description of Jesus in John as 'the Lamb of God who takes away the sin of the world' (1 vv 29; 36) has always been seen as a reference to his death. There is also an almost universal interpretation of that death as an atoning sacrifice 'putting things right with God'. Take, for example, the apparent cross-reference in I Peter (written around the end of the first century AD): 'You know that you were ransomed ... with the precious blood of Christ like that of a lamb without blemish or defect' (I Peter 1 v18). The term

'Lamb of God' has been used through the centuries by preachers and countless hymn-writers, to reinforce a doctrine of sacrificial atonement derived mainly from the teaching of Paul, mostly notably in his manifesto, the Letter to the Romans. This is a core Christian belief and that will not change!

However, it is the only phrase in all of John's Gospel which might bear that interpretation, with an echo of belief in atonement as such. And though it will forever be seen as such, the phrase is by no means a straightforward equivalent of what other New Testament writers and interpreters mean by sacrifice. From what we read in the rest of his Gospel, in which there is no hint of atonement as appeasement or ransom, if we approach the question afresh, what might John have meant by the term 'Lamb of God' which is used back in chapter 1 and not subsequently?

First, it is most likely to be a reference to the Passover. As we noted, John may actually have adjusted the date of the crucifixion to coincide with the killing of the Passover lambs across Jerusalem. In which case the reference is not so much to redemption (which the Passover was not) as to the triumphant mood of the Jews recalling the deliverance of their ancestors from captivity in Egypt by the Lord. John's principal clue is that the disciple Andrew's reaction to the Baptist's famous phrase is to tell his brother, 'we have found the Messiah' (1 v41). In contemporary thought that meant Conqueror and certainly not Victim. And although the Book of Revelation is no guide to understanding the thought of John the evangelist, we do read there of a Lamb, glorious after a triumph through suffering, who is the deliverer. When invited to look for the conquering Lion of Judah who can 'open the seals' (i.e. interpret the meaning of history) the writer can say 'Then I saw ... a Lamb standing as if it had been slaughtered' (Rev 5 v6). *Christus Victor* indeed. Second, some commentators link the term 'Lamb of God' with the Servant of the Lord who 'like a lamb that is led to the slaughter and, like a sheep that before its shearers is dumb, so he opened not his mouth' (Isaiah 53 v7); Actually Jesus is far from silent in John, unlike Mark 15 v5 or Matthew 27 v14. Already in its first decades, the Church was drawing parallels between Isaiah's suffering Servant of the Lord and the passion of Jesus as the Christ, presumably started by Jesus himself (Luke 24 vv25ff). Some of the various theories of the atonement owe their language to this parallel: 'it was the will of the Lord to crush him … and make his life an offering for sin' (Isaiah 53 v10). But John does not hint at this, though subsequent readers will forever make the connection and interpret 'Lamb of God' as a sacrifice. Again we must forgive J. S. Bach who uses it in his St Matthew Passion, though Matthew never uses this term.

Third, there is a possible cross-reference to the ram caught in a thicket which Abraham would substitute for his son Isaac whom he was about to kill (Genesis 22 vv9ff). In this interpretation Jesus is accepting death instead of us, but not as a 'payment' for our sins which the 'demand' for Isaac was not. The asymmetric parallel does not really work as it is Abraham who is being tested. Elsewhere, more generally in the cultic practices of the Jewish tradition, it was the blood of bulls and goats and calves, not lambs, which was deemed to take away sin (cf. Hebrews 9 vv11–14). In another traditional ritual it was a goat, the scapegoat, which was sent (un-killed) to take the people's sins away into the wilderness and to die there.

Lastly, if John's primary purpose is to proclaim that Jesus is the Messiah, the Christ, is it possible to find references to a lamb or ram as an image for the promised Messiah? Dodd has found one description of Judas Maccabeus as a great horned sheep in the book of Enoch, obscure now but maybe one with which Andrew, as a disciple of John the Baptist, might perhaps have been familiar.[58] Many who followed Jesus at first had nostalgia for the great Maccabean resurgence at the back of their minds. It is clear from the Synoptics that Jesus had to make a real effort to dispel this longing from his disciples' minds. In this he can scarcely be said to have succeeded, given that after the resurrection 'when they had come together they asked him "Lord, is this the time when you will restore the kingdom to Israel?"' (Acts 1 v6). Maybe the image of Jesus as the Passover lamb is John's version of the Messianic Secret – that Jesus was indeed the Christ but not the one that everyone was expecting. In all four Gospels Jesus was determined on his death from the feeding of the five thousand onwards, but for John this is a triumphal procession, not the 'march to the scaffold'.

In his autobiography C. S. Lewis recalls that he was familiar with many cultures in which the cycle of nature's annual renewal had been given a more or less religious or cultic interpretation of the dying and rising god. As he recalls, 'the hardest boiled of all the atheists I ever knew ... remarked that the evidence for the historicity of the Gospels was really surprisingly good. "Rum thing", he went on. "All that stuff of Frazer's about the Dying God. It almost looks as if it had really happened once"'.[59] John would agree; this story is nothing less than God's re-running of creation itself. This Lamb of God represents the triumph of God as creator and saviour. 'I have overcome the world' he says (16 v33).

Chapter 15

Blessed Assurance ...

From the close of Chapter 13 to the start of Chapter 18 John inserts an extended section of teaching about Jesus Christ with the main aim of reassurance. It begins with the familiar phrase 'let not your hearts be troubled' and concludes with 'take courage – I have overcome the world'. Rather like Matthew's so-called Sermon on the Mount (Chapters 5–7) in which the evangelist edits together a collection of Jesus' teaching on faith and practice, John has here drawn together his reflections on the meaning and message of Jesus Christ as it affects those who might be his followers, John's readers. The writing follows his usual literary style of ascribing most of the words to Jesus, though as throughout the book there is more commentary than verbatim record in the text.[60] It has even been suggested that this feature of John's style may result from it being the edited product of a series of sermons as the preacher presents Jesus and his message to the people. Maybe, but the lack of accurate quotation marks need not concern us at all. These chapters contain the heart of John's message to Christians and would-be Christians.

Many of John's first readers will have been asking the questions which the disciples ask (or are afraid to ask) in these chapters. How was Jesus the key to God's purpose of salvation? Who is he really? Will Jesus come back again? Where is he now? Are we really 'saved'? How can we tell? And these are questions still asked by thoughtful believers and would-be believers. John wants to reassure his readers through the teaching in these chapters with his central message, that if they 'trust in God' they should as well 'trust also in me' (14 v1). Dodd's approach is forthright: 'John has chosen to treat the death and resurrection as eschatological events. Christ's death on the cross *is* his ascent to the right hand of the Father, and his return to his disciples after death, which is closely associated if not identified with the coming of the Holy Spirit, *is* his second advent' (his italics).[61] So we have already witnessed 'the end of the world' if by that is meant the overcoming of the powers of darkness and despair and death; the life of the church at its best is the consolidation of that victory. There is nothing of the Synoptics' horror in Gethsemane, and certainly no hint of 'My God, my God, why hast thou forsaken me?' in this portrayal; there will be just a final triumphant word from the cross. John's Jesus is determined and confident – as John hopes his readers would be when trouble comes: 'I have said these things to keep you from stumbling' (16 v1). He is apprehensive, but as an expectant mother he looks beyond the pain (16 v21). As Dodd comments: 'It is true that the dramatic setting is that of "the night in which he was betrayed" with the crucifixion in prospect; yet in a real sense it is the risen and glorified Christ who speaks.'[62] This is the voice which John wants his readers to hear. This is the victorious Lord whom he wants them to believe in and identify with, hence the past tense 'I have overcome the world' (16 v33).[63] Jesus is anticipating the needs of his followers, as John will have known them when he wrote a generation or so later.

When Paul uses the metaphor of the body to describe the church, he does so to highlight the interdependence of each part on the others with Christ as the head. John here does something similar using the metaphor of the vine, familiar from the scriptures as meaning the People of God (Psalm 80 vv8ff; Isaiah 5 vv1–7; Mark 12 vv1–12). Jesus says 'I am the true vine and my Father is the vine-grower' (15 v1) who is about to prune the vine for the sake of new growth. It is as if the chosen people of Israel are now reduced to a single individual who will, after his glorious death and resurrection, grow again like a vine. This is as close as John ever comes to describing the disciples as the new Israel, though the word 'covenant' does not appear in John's

Gospel. There is a solidarity in Christ, analogous to what Paul calls the 'new creation' of the believers (II Corinthians 5 v17); this radical new beginning fulfils God's purpose in creation itself, 'when the fullness of time had come' (Galatians 4 v4).

Thus the section reflecting on the vine and the vineyard (15 vv1–11) is the claim by John that followers of Jesus are now the true People of God, heirs of all the promises providing they live the life of Christ's glory and love. There is in this metaphor an echo of the simpler teaching in the Sermon on the Mount (Matthew 7 v16ff): 'Beware of false prophets ... You will know them by their fruits.' The church is a continuation of the ministry of Jesus with the hallmark of fruit-bearing love. In the First Letter of John there is one of the most striking ways of putting this, echoing as it does the Prologue to the Gospel: 'No one has ever seen God; if we love one another, God lives in us and his love is perfected in us' (I John 4 v12). In chapters 14–17 of the Fourth Gospel the distinctive compassionate love (*agape*) of God comes to the fore: as Dodd points out,[64] there are 31 mentions of *agape* in these chapters, as compared to six in the earlier chapters.

The other great theme in these chapters is the phenomenon of the Holy Spirit in the lives of believers which is the life of God, the love of God which is the salvation of the world. This is for John, in effect, the continuing presence of the risen Jesus Christ. A few other New Testament passages echo this understanding: e.g., 'they attempted to go into Bithynia but the Spirit of Jesus did not allow them' (Acts 16 v7), or 'it is no longer I who live but Christ who lives in me' (Gal. 2 v20). For John this is central to his understanding of the resurrection and of the Holy Spirit. John describes the Holy Spirit as the '*Parakletos*' (14 v26) which is variously translated as Counsellor (RSV) or Advocate (NRSV) or Helper (GNB) or Champion (Sanders p. 326) or Comforter (KJV) or simply 'someone to stand by you' (J. B. Phillips). In later centuries scholars, rival bishops and church bureaucrats would wrestle with the vocabulary in which to affirm authentic belief in the Blessed Trinity. They had minimal help from John whose Jesus variously promises his disciples: 'Those who love me will keep my word and my Father will love them and we will come to them and make our home with them' (14 v23) or again 'the Holy Spirit whom the Father will send in my name' (14 v26) or again 'when the Advocate comes, whom I will send to you from the Father, the Spirit of truth who comes from the Father' (15 v26) or yet again 'the Spirit of truth ... will glorify me for he will take what is mine and declare it to you; all that the Father has is mine' (16 v14). In the light of these and other verses, if it had not become so deadly serious, the later arguments about the *filioque* in the creeds (as to whether the Spirit proceeds from the Father and the Son) would be almost entertaining.[65]

John is unclear precisely because the Spirit, like the wind (3 v8), cannot be pinned down and certainly not defined in a dogmatic text. For John the experience of the Holy Spirit was to be what Charles Wesley calls 'the witness of Jesus returned to his home'.[66] There is nothing here of the phenomena of 'spiritual gifts', sometimes eccentric, which Paul had to deal with (I Corinthians 12–14). Love is enough – as of course it was for Paul who overrides the claims about such gifts with his hymn of praise to *agape* (I Corinthians 13). After the resurrection, echoing the creation story (Genesis 2 v7) John has Jesus breathing the breath of life, the Holy Spirit, into his disciples, to raise them from the dust to be spiritually alive with his resurrection life (20 v22). He would have echoed the affirmation at the close of Matthew's Gospel, 'I am with you always, to the end of this age', and meant by that the presence of the Holy Spirit. If there are fruits, then there is the Spirit at work, much as the trees move as evidence of the wind. In the familiar refrain from Taizé, *'ubi caritas et amor, ibi deus est'*, ('where there is compassionate love, God is there').

The overall impact of these chapters is what matters. As we saw, readings from John have always posed a difficulty for compilers of lectionaries; the natural length of each episode is often a full chapter, too long for reading in church. This is especially true of Chapters 14–16, with Chapter 17 as a distinct but related section too; any extracted passage loses the sense of the whole. All 90 plus verses are needed for John to spell out the core characteristics of Jesus' own message and the inheritance of his followers. The motifs are woven together, community and friendship, departure and return, persecution and determination, rejection and reward. These four reflective chapters are inserted into the narrative flow from 13 v38 to 18 v1. They represent a lifetime of reflection and meditation by John on the phenomenon of Jesus as Christ, showing us the Father, signalled in the Prologue and now spelt out with great care. John writes from the heart about the centrality of love and of the promised joy of a Christian life, of death and resurrection analogous to childbirth, which will soon be a reality for the believers. But above all John seeks to instil a sense of reassurance as Jesus calls his disciples friends, though he knows that even Simon Peter will deny him (13 vv36–38)). 'I have said these things to you so that in me you may have peace' (16 v33), foreshadowing the greeting on Easter evening 'Peace be with you' (20 v19).

It is a powerful presentation, aimed at several different contemporary readerships: the intimate confidential atmosphere in the room would have appealed to those who might otherwise have taken a non-Christian Gnostic or 'mystical' path; the freshness of the presentation of God as Father of all would have appealed to Jews who were sad or frustrated or angry at the collapse of their own religious system in a flurry of nationalism; the determined integrity of the hero might have appealed to those who admired such virtues in, say, Socrates; the call to unity would have rung bells with those uneasy or unhappy about divisions among Christians. Above all the focus on *agape*, generous love, as the key to forgiveness and behaviour would have appealed to those readers who, more generally, were searching for a meaning and purpose in their lives and relationships. It is the person of Jesus, Messiah and Emmanuel, now at hand through the Spirit for every believer, which is his good news. John's anticipation of his readers' needs is essentially reassuring, light in darkness, hope in crisis, a timeless message with a perennial appeal.

Chapter 16

One Flock, One Shepherd

John shares with Paul a concern for the unity of the Christian church, perhaps born of controversy in a local congregation or of disputes across a wider field. Paul lambasts the Corinthians for their disunity – while addressing them as 'called to be saints' (I Cor. 1 v2)! In particular their practice of celebrating what he calls 'the Lord's supper' is scandalous: 'In this matter I do not commend you' (I Cor. 11 v22). He then introduces the metaphor of the body with each part required for the proper functioning of the whole. His letters are forever pleading for authentic togetherness in Christ and in the Spirit.

John is equally concerned for the unity of Christians. In the familiar words of Chapter 17, the foundation text of the ecumenical movement, we read: 'I ask not only on behalf of these *(his immediate disciples)*, but also on behalf of those who will believe in me through their word, that they may all be one. As you, Father, are in me and I am in you, may they also be in us, so that the world may believe that you have sent me' (17 vv20–21). The unity of believers is set forth as evidence of the truth of the gospel, a persuasive phenomenon which may lead 'the world' to believe in the identity of Jesus Christ.

However, from the beginning and into our own time, Christians have argued passionately about whether disunity in itself does in fact dishonour the gospel, or whether the reverse is sometimes the case. There are beliefs or attitudes or practices which necessarily divide the church because they are seen by some to be incompatible with Christianity as it is known and practised at any particular time. In the early centuries there were several bitter divisions over doctrine and practice. Some of what we may with hindsight consider to be 'resurrection moments' in church history derive from crises of intentional disunity, from the early centuries through a period such as the Reformation down to more recent times. Successful and unsuccessful reformers alike are derided, or worse, from within the mainstream for the divisions they created and the trouble and even the bloodshed. Pioneers or heretics? One thing is clear: there is a strange and profound asymmetry between those who affirm that the truth of the gospel overrides the unity of the church and those who believe that the unity of the church is itself the truth of the gospel. This dilemma is as much a challenge today as ever it was at any crunch point in church history.

John is surely aware of this when he takes us further: 'The glory that you have given me I have given them, so that they may be one, as we are one, I in them and you in me, that they may become completely one, so that the world may know that you have sent me and have loved them even as you have loved me' (17 vv22–23). Only when we recall what John means by the 'glory' of Jesus are we brought up short by this verse which otherwise flows past in an ecumenical haze. The cross is the demonstration of glory in John's interpretation. It is in laying down his life (10 v11; 15 v13) that Jesus is glorified and his God-given role defined. A unity among Christians which is not built on a willingness to love and serve, sacrificially and unconditionally, will not fulfil the prayer of John 17. The world will believe not when the Churches are visibly united but when more Christians are Christ-like! And to be fair, this is what many Churches are affirming when they bundle together 'Mission and Unity' within their organisations.

In one of the few parables in John, Jesus draws on the imagery of the shepherd and the sheep (10 vv1ff). Even here it is more a metaphor than a true parable such as those which abound in the Synoptics. Jesus is the good shepherd who protects, feeds and generally looks after his flock, to the point of laying down his life for the sheep. One might ask, somewhat tongue in cheek, whether the shepherd does this because he owns the sheep or because he loves them? But for John, who has left the literal metaphor far behind, the two are the same: we belong to Jesus who loves us, and this is what constitutes the unity of Christians. There are 'other sheep' who also belong to Jesus (10 v16) though they are not of the (Jewish) fold, as John well knew by the time he was writing. There will be one flock only because there is one shepherd. 'I know my own and my own know me ... they will listen to my voice' (10 vv14, 16).

We need to remember, given the reliance on quotes from John which sustained the twentieth-century ecumenical movement, that he is not actually saying that Christian unity is about church structures, as though it were an organisational matter. It is rather *koinonia*, belonging together in community or communion, one flock in many folds, which the most thoughtful ecumenists have of course always affirmed. In the first century 'other folds' would simply mean other places and different cultures. For example, the letters to seven churches set out in Revelation Chapters 2 and 3 are all addressed to 'the church in X' and similarly Paul's letters are addressed collectively to all the Christians in, for example, Corinth or Philippi. This may mean that all the Christians in each city might have constituted a single fellowship, albeit in separate 'house churches'. Who knows? But to the letter-writers, Paul and the John of Revelation, they are clearly deemed to be a unit, one 'something', in Revelation deserving of collective praise or blame. Strictly speaking the term *ekklesia* (which became the normal Greek word for church) means either 'a gathered group (congregation) of Christians worshipping together' or 'the total number of Christians across the centuries and around the world'; all other uses of the word church are provisional and temporary.[67] Of course for us there is no turning back the clock to that first century, replicating the hundreds of small towns and cities where all the Christians probably did know one another. But the contemporary terminology of 'Churches Together in X' or 'Christians Together in X' does seem closer to John's theology of Christian unity than some of the 'schemes for union' which regard diversity as a problem however much they protest otherwise.[68]

The unity which is described in John, with his metaphor of one shepherd, was vulnerable. From the outset such a powerful and persuasive movement as Christianity soon attracted imitators as we saw in an earlier chapter, not least those who brought one or more characteristics of their previous religious beliefs with them. The First Letter of John is full of warnings about Christian unity being sabotaged by these new-comers. As we saw, some may have had dealings with Mithraism, may have dabbled in some form of 'mystery religion' or been affected by Gnosticism. Converts from groups such as these may have thought that Christianity was another similar religion built around 'mystery', the inside track to paradise beloved of esoteric groups and cults for thousands of years before and since. And in a time of persecution, the Christians did necessarily meet in secret to share 'the body and blood' in what might have sounded like dubious practice. The First Letter of John is blunt: 'this is the message you have heard from the beginning, that we should love one another ... we know love by this, that he laid down his life for us ... and we ought to lay down our lives for one another' (I John 3 vv11, 17). And in the very next verse he presses the point: 'Let us love not in word or speech but in truth and action.' This is all in the spirit of John's Gospel. Believing in Jesus requires active love rather than religious or quasi-religious rituals. True Christian unity is not a cosy club or an in-crowd huddling together out of the public gaze performing special rituals en route for heaven – a phenomenon not unknown today! Rather it is a communion (*koinonia*), a true community of the faithful who are authentic disciples in thought, word and deed of Jesus the Christ for whom glory meant laying down his life to demonstrate God's love. This Saviour was no Socrates, whose uncompromising intellectual rigour had led him to something approaching suicide, albeit honourably under the law. For John, though he appears to be well aware of the diversity of contemporary philosophies and religious or spiritual practices, the 'way and truth and life' was at heart the willing self-sacrifice of one who reckoned that only through his death would the glory of God be known. Only thus might the will of God, the love of God, be fulfilled, as followers of Jesus Christ might take forward not his ideas only but his attitude and his spirit.

To repeat: the world will believe not just when the churches are visibly united but when Christians are Christ-like. As for authentic *koinonia*, how true is the saying: those who draw near to Christ draw near to those who draw near to Christ. This elusive stance, derived from the crucial invitation 'follow me', is sufficient to define Christian unity as John understands it. Would that it sufficed us.

Chapter 17

In Spirit and in Truth

There is no doubting the single-mindedness of John in presenting Jesus as the Christ, the 'one who is to come', the incarnate Son of God, so that salvation is a recognition of this identity. This leads him inevitably to an apparently exclusive message, 'No one comes to the Father but by me' (14 v6).

This text, usually quoted out of context, has caused many Christians to exclude all non-Christians from any hope of salvation – and sometimes to exclude any Christians different from themselves! Certainly John is at pains to castigate the Jewish authorities for their non-recognition of God's saving act. But how does this square with his affirmation in the Prologue that 'the true light, which enlightens everyone, was coming into the world' (1 v9)? Who is walking in that light? What are we to make of exclusive claims in a world of many faiths?

Again we need to remember that John's own world was full of religious diversity. Though he drew on a limited range of personal testimonies from those who witnessed the events he is interpreting, he is clearly aware of a wider spread of religious convictions and communities which formed the context of Christian preaching. C. H. Dodd gives an exhaustive account of the many strands of contemporary thinking and belief which can be discerned in John's Gospel.[69] They may not have been the global religions and faith traditions of our own times but, as John seeks to relate to his hoped-for many readers, his vocabulary and ideas resonate with a wide variety of expectations and experiences. In commenting on Jesus' encounter with the Samaritan woman John writes, 'the hour is coming – and is now here – when the true worshippers will worship the Father in spirit and in truth, for the Father seeks such as these to worship him. God is spirit and those who worship him must worship in spirit and in truth' (4 vv23f). It is almost as if the intense intimacy of the believer's relationship with God overcomes all attempts at organised religion!

It is certainly true that inter-religious dialogue depends on a respect for both spirit and truth if it is to be meaningful and helpful to the participants. There must be an openness to the 'spirit' and an acknowledgment that all parties to a dialogue are open to that spirit which is known, as John says, by its effect like trees blown by the wind (3 v8). But a spiritual openness is not enough; there must also be 'truth'. For John, it is important to remember, 'truth' is far removed from dogma or propositional affirmation; rather it is relational, the utter authenticity of the person of Jesus Christ, the one who has made the Father known, the touchstone of truth for Christians. We believe that God is Christ-like, says John, so we approach along that way. It is not believers who 'define' God – for that is inherently impossible – but rather we believe it is God who has made himself knowable. Hence John can affirm Jesus as the way, the truth and the life with no contradiction of his earlier affirmation that 'in him was life and the life was the light of all people' (1 v5). The incarnation allows us to believe without arrogance. 'What is being said here … is that Jesus is in fact the presence of God's truth and God's life in the world, and that to know the Father means to follow the way which Jesus is', as Lesslie Newbigin puts it.[70] Coming from a leader of the twentieth-century ecumenical movement this interpretation is far from the exclusiveness (and occasional triumphalism) which often characterised the eighteenth- and nineteenth-century global missionary movement as part of European colonialism.

As John puts it: 'For this I was born and for this I came into the world, to testify to the truth. Everyone who belongs to the truth listens to my voice' (18 38ff). This is 'in spirit and in truth' again. What John means by 'everyone … listens to my voice' seems to be as inclusive as 'whoever comes to me I will never turn away' (6 v17). So, for example, it is significant that many of the core statements on ethics which are attributed to Jesus are universally acknowledged, just as we saw that guidance built on the so-called Golden Rule is found in all the major faith traditions and their scriptures. However, for John Jesus is not essentially a moral teacher, so John would not be satisfied with this interpretation of 'listening to my voice'. 'Believe in God; believe also in me' is the focal point of John's message (14 v1).

So what of non-Christian believers in God? It simply can never be determined whether or how Jesus of Nazareth intended 'Christianity' to emerge as the world religion it soon became, even as his disciples were being sent 'into all the world' to teach and baptise (Matthew 28 v20). What can at least be stated is that the Jesus of the Gospels, and certainly John's Jesus, would not have wanted the aggressive or abusive practices against other world faiths which have featured in his name over the centuries, as Christians have sought, often desperately, in Paul's words, 'by any means to save some' (I Corinthians 9 v22). For John especially, for whom faith was such a personal commitment, there would surely have been serious question marks against the practice of a whole tribe adopting Christianity when their ruler did so.[71]He might well have challenged the practice of parents 'christening' their innocent (and of course uncommitted) infants. The least one can say, in the spirit of John, is that, given that the Church contains unbelievers, he might have gone on to acknowledge that there are 'believers' outside the Church, if by that is meant those who believe that God is Christ-like after the pattern of Christ-likeness set out in his Gospel. Perhaps 'those who have not seen and yet have come to believe' who are blessed (20 v29) also includes many of those who have never even heard.

As to dialogue between committed believers of different faiths, John can have nothing direct to say. Such encounters are the product of the globalisation of the last five or six hundred years, accelerating into our own time. Back in the first century cities were market places for ideas as much as for goods and services. Hence Paul could get a mixed crowd in the market squares, including the famous occasion in Athens (Acts 17 vv16ff). But this was not 'inter-faith encounter' as we now know it. Nowadays all European cities contain communities and worship centres of several active faith communities. Paradoxically, society looks to religion to be a unifying element across society and even internationally, while at the same time wondering and worrying about the damage it does! A former chief rabbi, Jonathan Sacks, described inter-faith relations as 'face to face and side by side' which is true, provided you do the 'side by side' bit first. When those of different persuasions unite around a common cause, trust is established which allows us to share more deeply, face to face. As Rowan Williams said in a radio broadcast, we need to ask our partners in dialogue 'what can you see from there?'.[72] John would surely have agreed, knowing how readily all righteousness slips into self-righteousness and all claims to being 'God's chosen people' become blinkered to the point of blindness (9 vv35ff). John allows for spiritual development, within the parameters of belief in the Christ-like God, and indeed expects it: 'I still have many things to say to you but you cannot bear them now. When the Spirit of truth comes, he will guide you into all the truth' (16 v12). Spirit and truth again; the essential elements of all faith and all faiths. Dare we say, always humbly (for even this can be stated with a false or patronising self-confidence), that the Christ-like God can be unknowingly known in faiths other than Christianity? Maybe. John's words are strong: in Jesus of Nazareth 'the true light which enlightens everyone was coming into the world' (1 v9).

Chapter 18

'What I Have Written ...'

The kingly status of Jesus is a main theme throughout John. But, curiously perhaps, apart from the Passion narrative, the term 'kingdom' is only mentioned twice (in the story of the meeting with Nicodemus, 3 vv3' 5) as compared with dozens of mentions of the kingdom in the Synoptics, especially in the 'parables of the kingdom' (e.g., Matthew 13). Even so, John is no less clear that Jesus is inaugurating a kingdom with a king, and that this is at the heart of his identity. His enemies try to modify the inscription on the cross with the words 'he claimed to be ...' but Pilate will have none of it (19 v22). According to John the charge said 'King of the Jews' in Latin and Greek and Hebrew, a detail which the main manuscripts of the Synoptics do not mention. Pilate wanted everyone, including visitors to the city at Festival time, to know. The thrust of the dialogue between Jesus and Pilate is about being a king, around what constitutes power. But Pilate is clear; he will not change what he had written.

This issue is at the heart of the ministry of Jesus: what is this kingdom, and, especially in John, what is Jesus' status as a king? This has its roots in one of the definitive episodes in Jesus' ministry. John alone provides us with the vital clue to the mystery surrounding the feeding of the five thousand. The Synoptics offer what seems a straightforward miracle story, but John's account is required for us to appreciate what it meant politically. When Jesus moved to Galilee to develop his ministry he soon became extremely popular, preaching and healing around the many small towns and villages. At one point the crowds were so dense that four men bringing a paralysed friend for healing had to open a hole in the roof to lower him down to Jesus. The words of the King James Version are amusingly memorable, 'they could not come nigh unto him for the press' (Mark 2 v2); Jesus drew great crowds (but no press!). The Synoptics describe the five thousand as one such crowd listening to a celebrity and in some cases hoping for a healing. But John gives us the key to what was instead a highly politically charged moment. Jesus faces down a legion of men who want him as their anointed king (6 v15).

Popularity had led more than one firebrand to be hailed as Messiah, start a rebellion and be crushed and crucified by the Roman authorities. The chronology is unclear but the uprising of 'Judas the Galilean' may have been around 6 AD, very possibly witnessed by the young Jesus. In the Acts of the Apostles another rebellion, led by Theudas, is placed earlier than Jesus' time, though the date cannot be certain. What is clear is that there was a mood across the land of impatience and sometimes outrage and violence. The prisoner Barabbas, in custody at the same time as Jesus, is described by Mark (15 v7) as having 'committed murder during the insurrection'. John describes him as a 'bandit' which is the word for an activist in an uprising. This was not an uprising or insurrection that made the history books. There must have been several groups, more or less outlaws, roaming round like guerrilla fighters, doing what damage they could to the Roman occupying forces.

The phenomenon of John the Baptist is part of this sense of crisis. His message is of national renewal, a cleansing by way of preparation for the coming judgement, to which thousands of people responded. The Roman occupation had impoverished and humiliated a proud people; taxes were heavy and petty oppression frequent – all empires are like this, ancient and modern. Much like the so-called Arab Spring of 2011/2012, there was a deep sense that change was in the air, that oppression might be overcome. John the Baptist himself is challenged in John (though not in the Synoptics) as to whether he is himself the Messiah; in all four gospels he is clear that he is only the forerunner. Someone is coming who will change everything, someone whom John's disciples such as Andrew will call the Messiah from Chapter 1 'the one who is to come'. Jewish expectations of the 'one who is to come' at that time were derived from the glorious story of the Maccabee father and sons, who secured national sovereignty across Judaea from around 164 BC to 63 BC. The Messiah would be king and saviour, son of David, victor and liberator, faithful and strong.

It is the execution of John the Baptist which triggers the gathering of the five thousand men. Matthew adds 'besides women and children' not understanding the politics of the event; they would have been almost all men. The five thousand sit down in fifties and hundreds, looking just like a legion waiting for orders. The forerunner is gone; now it is time for the one who is to come. And then it is over. The miracle of the feeding disguises for us – and maybe for the Synoptic writers too – the critical nature of the event. John tells us, 'When the people saw the sign that he had done they began to say "this is indeed the prophet who is to come into the world". When Jesus realised that they were about to come and take him by force to make him king, he withdrew again to the mountain by himself' (6, vv14f).

Dare we attribute to Jesus a change of perspective at that moment, as he wrestled in prayer or was tempted afresh as in the desert some months before? He has in effect turned the stones into bread, he has glimpsed the power that could come with his own powers and has agonised over the crowd 'like sheep without a shepherd', needing leadership. For John, Jesus has not come to change the world other than changing people. No wonder the rest of Chapter 6 is all about his own identity in very otherworldly language, deliberately rejecting the earthly Messianic opportunity. It is in these often mysterious verses that John introduces the references to the later Christian celebration of the Eucharist rather than in his account of the Last Supper. 'Very truly I tell you, unless you eat the flesh of the Son of Man and drink his blood you have no life in you' (6 v53). Incidentally, these strong words might well have triggered the charge of some form of cannibalism which was later laid against Christians.[73] It is at this point, the turning point of Jesus' ministry, that some of his disciples 'turned back and no longer went about with him' (6 v66). So dare we see even Jesus himself human enough to have changed his priorities about proclaiming the kingdom? Jesus asked the twelve 'do you also wish to go away?' and Simon Peter answered him 'Lord, to whom can we go? You have the words of eternal life!' (6, vv67f). Peter is almost ministering to Jesus as a friend with these words of loyalty. After this episode Jesus concentrated on teaching his close disciples and not on popular preaching to large crowds. There is thereafter almost nothing about the kingdom until we reach the last days. But John's extended dialogues with Pilate across Chapters 18 and 19 are all about Jesus as king. In dramatic style they show three interested parties all trying to achieve their goals, Jesus, Pilate and the Jewish leaders.

At the heart of it Jesus himself is determined to go through to his death and will now do nothing to stop that happening: 'there is no greater love than this, to lay down one's life for one's friends' (15 v13). This is, for John, where the glory of God will be revealed. As we saw, to describe the crucifixion as 'being lifted up' (3 v14; 12 v32) John uses the word for enthronement or coronation. At the last, Jesus is determined to be crowned. In the final conversation (19 vv8ff) Jesus in effect rebukes Pilate's claim to absolute authority by reminding him that even he is answerable to Caesar (and of course, for John, to God). This reminder is reinforced in the very next paragraph when the Jewish leaders accuse Pilate of *'maiestas'*, disloyalty to Caesar. Commentators note that in 33 AD Pilate's patron in Rome, Tiberius's chief-of-staff Sejanus, was dismissed, disgraced and killed on this charge.[74] Jesus knows that he is the king and must fulfil his destiny and role.

Secondly, the Jewish leaders are determined to be rid of Jesus, fearful lest his popularity turn into a movement which might bring down ruin on them all. This fear was correct: the unrest across the land after another 30 years would become outright rebellion leading to the destruction of Jerusalem by the Romans. They appear to have done some kind of deal overnight, though maybe not with Pilate himself. When Pilate formally asks (as in all Roman courts) what the charges are, they remind him of the arrangement 'if he were not a criminal we would not have handed him over to you'. This disingenuous statement clearly rankles the governor; it was after all very early in the morning! So he proceeds to interrogate the prisoner and their plan unravels as Pilate sees a chance to outwit and humiliate them.

For Pilate has his own agenda. From other sources we learn that he is far from the weak character depicted in Matthew as washing his hands, metaphorically and literally. As the charges mount from 'claiming to be Messiah' through 'claiming to be a king' to 'claiming to be son of God' the tension also mounts. Despite the political and personal sensitivity of being accused of considering an acquittal and allowing Jesus to get away with being king – and thus 'opposing Caesar' – the wily old colonial governor actually ends up with a win. Eventually the chief priests answered 'we have no king but Caesar', which for Pilate is gratifying grovelling and for John is the ultimate blasphemy in the mouths of Jewish leaders. 'Then he handed him over to be crucified' (19 vv15ff). And some time later he proceeds to rub it in 'what I have written stays written'. This is your king, meaning 'this is my opinion of you'.

John's masterly dramatisation of these encounters demonstrates the centrality in his presentation of the opening editorial comment: 'he came unto his own and his own received him not' (1 v11). What appears as the 'Messianic secret' in the Synoptics is more subtly handled here, though it is also the substance of the charges made in the Synoptics' accounts of the trial. For John as we have seen, apart from one episode in

Chapter 7, there is no real prohibition laid on the disciples, no secret. From first to last it is John's purpose to present Jesus as the Christ, the Messiah, the 'anointed one', from 1 v41 to 20 v31. Jesus is paraded before the crowd in his purple (kingly) robe (19 v5) whereas in Mark this robe is simply a backstairs taunt of the soldiers.

Nor is 'of the Jews' in the inscription on the cross straightforward. Pilate means it as an insult to the little local people with whom he has to deal, like so many high-handed colonial military governors before and since. 'Am I a Jew?' Pilate exclaims when Jesus suggests that the question 'Are you the king of the Jews?' has been planted for him to ask. When Jesus says 'My kingdom is not of this world' he goes on to say 'if my kingdom were from this world, my followers would be fighting to keep me from being handed over *to the Jews*' [my italics]. At one level this is another attempt to minimise the shame of Jesus' death by crucifixion on the part of gospel writers who are, by the time of writing, well aware that it raises serious questions when Christians are preaching across the Roman Empire. Blaming the Jews was needed in the first century – but proved tragic and disgraceful later. At a deeper level John is reminding us of the core claims by Christians that Jesus was indeed the fulfilment of ancient promises made to the Jews and recorded in their scriptures. By the time the gospels were written the Greek word 'Christ' was Jesus' name rather than his title, as it still is. Thus 'Christ the King' is strictly speaking a tautology. He is the 'Messiah' with saving, kingly power far beyond the Jews.

Chapter 19

'Supposing Him to Be the Gardener'

There is one unlikely Greek noun which occurs in two episodes in John's Gospel and nowhere else in the New Testament, the word for 'garden'. When Jesus and his disciples go out of the city after the meal they cross the brook Kidron (as David famously did during the rebellion of Absalom in 2 Samuel 15) and enter a garden. They must have done this many times, as of course David had, but this time was very special, marking a crisis of kingship, again as for David. The Synoptics all name the place Gethsemane, though they do not call it a garden. The place now believed to be Gethsemane is a strange, evocative olive grove at the foot of the Mount of Olives, with some trees dating back nearly 2,000 years. The fact that John does not use the local name Gethsemane, given his awareness of so many detailed local memories of Jerusalem Christians, draws this comment from Dodd: 'The whole matter is trivial and for that reason it appears to me one of the strongest pieces of evidence we have yet found that John was here writing in independence of Mark, and yet on the basis of good information.'[75]

But the use of the word 'garden' may also be symbolic, although Sanders in his commentary calls the following suggestion 'perhaps too ingenious to imagine';[76] anyway, here it is. At the beginning of the Prologue John deliberately echoes the opening of the book of Genesis 'in the beginning'. The phenomenon of Jesus Christ is the new creation, renewing all the original divine gifts of light and life and love. And so this garden represents the reversal of that Genesis garden, Eden, where 'Man's first disobedience and the fruit of that forbidden tree whose mortal taste brought death into the world – and all our woe', as John Milton begins 'Paradise Lost'. Jesus is now determined on the final hours of his life. The true enemy whom

Jesus now confronts is not Judas but 'the ruler of this world' (14 v30). Of this enemy Jesus has said, 'He has no power over me but I do as the Father has commanded me, so that the world may know that I love the Father' (14 v31). This does seem like a commentary on the story of the serpent in Eden. Jesus' obedience will overcome Adam's disobedience, for our salvation. He is for John as well as for Paul a 'second Adam' (I Corinthians 15 v45). Jesus obeys the summons of the authorities as the summons of his Father. Even though Jesus' obedience is not hard-won as in the Synoptics – when 'his sweat became like great drops of blood falling down on the ground' (Luke 22 v44) – it is still obedience, and Jesus is the champion taking on the enemy. The cross itself will be the victory which is already assured: 'I have overcome the world' (16 v33).

The Blessed John Henry Newman puts it so well in the 'Dream of Gerontius':

O loving wisdom of our God! When all was sin and shame
a second Adam to the fight and to the rescue came.
O wisest love, that flesh and blood which did in Adam fail
should strive afresh against the foe, should strive and
should prevail.
O generous love, that he who smote in man for man the foe,
the double agony in man for man should undergo;
and in the garden secretly, and on the cross on high,
should teach his brethren, and inspire to suffer and to die.[77]

Secondly, John is the only one to describe the location of the tomb of Jesus as in a garden. In the Synoptics the tomb is new, belonging to Joseph of Arimathea. John's story adds Nicodemus, also a rich and influential man and a member of the Sanhedrin, and the two of them organise the embalming and the burial, again presumably on land belonging to one of them. Maybe they intended later to move the body to a more suitable memorial place with a proper tomb. The place of execution was 'outside the city wall' and so its actual location has been contested because the city wall had been broken and rebuilt at least twice since the time of King David. The line of the wall was adjusted more than once during the decades of Roman rule before being effectively lost when the city was flattened after the rebellion in 70 AD.

The Synoptics give no detail about the relationship or distance between Golgotha and the tomb. John alone is clear, presumably from his Jerusalem sources: 'Now there was a garden in the place where he was crucified and in the garden there was a new tomb ...' (19 v41). On the basis of this verse the mighty Church of the Holy Sepulchre was built to comprise two main sections, Calvary and the tomb, adjacent to each other under one complex roof, to mark the spot. Perhaps surprisingly, this claim is very probable though not, of course, certain. According to Eusebius of Caesarea, 'The Roman emperor Hadrian in the 2nd century AD built a temple dedicated to the goddess Aphrodite in order to bury the cave in which Jesus had been buried.'[78] It was this temple which Constantine demolished in 325 AD, to allow for the building of the first church on the site, which was described as 'a basilica of wondrous beauty' by a pilgrim as early as 333 AD.[79] This sequence is plausible, at least as likely as the site of the basilica of St Peter in Rome (also started by Constantine) marking his grave.

But of course John the evangelist's concern is not really with 'where' or 'how' but with 'who' and 'why'. Here is where the temporary nature of the death of Jesus as Christ is confirmed, a uniquely special place. This becomes the Easter garden, a place of new life, of hope after despair, of all the stones rolled away, with possibilities so mind-blowing that God himself might be walking in this garden in the cool of the day, a new paradise garden. And there is a gardener who calls the reader by name as the dawn breaks: 'Mary', he says, or whatever your name might be, reader. The one who has won through all this for you is inviting you to believe, to follow and to live.

Chapter 20

Touching!

There is an irony in the tradition that Thomas ended up in India preaching to mystics, given that his moment in the spotlight finds him protesting that the resurrection of Jesus cannot be a real, actual and physical event: 'unless I see and touch I will not believe' (20 v25). Despite his nickname, 'doubting' Thomas was not a sceptic, just a realist.

Thomas is included every time the Twelve are listed in the Synoptics, including the last list at Pentecost; he is presumably from Galilee though there is no account of his call. He goes fishing with Peter in John Chapter 21. His name derives from the Aramaic meaning 'twin' which is why he was called Didymus (the Greek for twin). He speaks twice earlier in John (but nowhere in the Synoptics), once to encourage the disciples to go with Jesus back to Judea despite the mounting danger (11 v16) and once on the final evening when he blurts out 'Lord, we do not know where you are going, so how can we know the way?' (14 v5). This is hardly a rounded character study, though it does suggest a man who would be likely to ask for evidence and do so in the blunt manner quoted.

But as with most of the Twelve he disappears from view in subsequent accounts. Tradition has it that he sailed east to Muziris, in south-western India (Kerala) around 50 AD. This was apparently a thriving port, though its precise location is now uncertain, and Pliny the Elder, 20 years later, advised against landing there as it was full of brigands – clearly Thomas had not converted them all! In his description of apostolic mission fields, Eusebius (early fourth century) has Thomas as the missionary to the Parthians, Rome's persistent enemy on its eastern border. So despite this somewhat contrived attempt to describe the apostolic outreach as 'truly global', there may be truth in Thomas having gone to the East. For what it is worth Marco Polo records visiting Thomas' tomb.[80] There are certainly 'Saint Thomas Christians' across India, who worship in Syriac (a language close to Aramaic) and are often called Nazrani, followers of the Nazarene.

Thomas is an unlikely choice to make the ultimate – and for John definitive – affirmation about Jesus, 'my Lord and my God' (20 v28). This honour might have fallen to Peter or 'the Beloved Disciple' or perhaps Andrew (giving a neat symmetry with his first declaration of Jesus' identity as Messiah in 1 v41). But Thomas it was – and doubters have taken heart ever since! For as John Marsh notes: 'The words "my Lord" would have sufficed to show that Thomas was now as satisfied as any other of the disciples that Jesus had returned to them; in adding the words "and my God" he is taking a step beyond the relationship between disciple and rabbi.'[81] Though invited to 'put your finger here and see my hands' John does not record whether he did so. But he does record the comment of Jesus: 'blessed are those who have not seen but are yet believing (trusting)' (20 vv26ff). A later writer would comment: 'though you have not seen him, you love him' (I Peter 1 v8). These particular words of Thomas 'my Lord and my God' may have been set down by John as a challenge to the emperor Domitian (81–96) in whose time there was serious persecution of Christians. Some historians have claimed that Domitian demanded to be known as *Dominus et Deus* (Lord and God) though there is no coinage to back up that suggestion. But not since the opening verses ('and the Word was God') has Jesus Christ actually been called God, except by his critics and enemies (e.g., 10 vv31ff). For John's first readers, worship is being regularly offered to Jesus as Lord and God. Thus Pliny the Younger, as a provincial governor, has a comment in his celebrated letter to the emperor Trajan.[82] He asks advice on what to do about Christians who 'asserted that the sum and substance of their fault or error had been that they were accustomed to meet on a fixed day before dawn and sing responsively a hymn to Christ as to a god'. If the whole Gospel of John is, in part, a confidence-building exercise then this outburst by Thomas is the climax to the story, the affirmation which will ensure life 'in all its fullness' (10 v10). It mirrors the prologue perfectly.

The other unique Easter story in the Fourth Gospel concerns Mary Magdalene. Let C. H. Dodd have the first word:

This story never came out of any common stock of tradition ... Either we have a free, imaginative composition based upon the bare tradition of an appearance to Mary Magdalene ... or else the story came through some highly individual channel directly from the source. ... The power to render psychological traits imaginatively with convincing insight cannot be denied to a writer to whom we owe the masterly character-parts of Pontius Pilate and the Woman of Samaria. Yet I cannot for long rid myself of the feeling ... that this has something indefinably first-hand about it. There is nothing like it in the gospels. Is there anything quite like it in all ancient literature?[83]

As Thomas is bidden to touch, Mary is forbidden. Even to ask why this should be so is to take a risk. On the face of it, since John understands the resurrection and ascension as a single episode, the words 'do not hold on to me' mean that John believes that the bodily resurrection appearances are temporary and that the time is now near when Jesus will be 'accessible' to all, 'not seeing but believing' (20 v29). Thus William Temple: 'Our devotion is not to hold us by the empty tomb; it must lift our hearts to heaven.'[84] To see Jesus means, for John, to appreciate what God was doing in and through him. Thus when some Greeks want to see Jesus, he cries out 'the hour has come for the Son of Man to be glorified' (12 v23) since John is presenting Jesus as the Saviour of the whole world.

The risk is, of course, to deduce from this encounter that

Mary Magdalene was more likely than any other person to cling to Jesus. She lingers alone in the garden, weeping like a widow; her name is spoken in that unforgettable way. It is on such atmospheric texts that the whole flimsy hypothesis of Jesus' relationship with her, even marriage, is dependent – a matter unmentionable by the formal commentators of course! Allusions to Mary being close to Jesus were actively suppressed by orthodox believers during subsequent centuries even as the rumours persisted (see the postscript below). However, it cannot be denied that the Greek word describing her contact may rightly be translated 'grasp' or 'cling'. It is definitely stronger than merely 'touch' (as in the Latin *noli me tangere*) and once or twice in other literature even means 'kindle into flame'.

Mary Magdalene is mentioned a dozen times in all four gospels, more often than any disciple other than the closest three, Peter and the brothers James and John. Given the rather large number of Marys around, there has been confusion from the beginning as to whether this Mary was the sister of Martha and Lazarus. Luke thinks not, but that she was one of the Galilean women who accompanied Jesus from early days and whom he had healed 'from whom seven demons had gone out' (Luke 8 v2). But John implies that Mary the sister of Martha had good reason to thank Jesus for some kindness and forgiveness; he identifies her as 'the one who anointed the Lord with perfume and wiped his feet with her hair' (11 v2; 12 vv1–8). Since Pope Gregory (590 AD) several imaginative commentators, novelists and dramatists (notably Dorothy L. Sayers[85]) have conflated the two characters into one. In the Synoptics Mary Magdalene heads the various lists of women at the cross and bringing the spices to the tomb. In John she comes alone to the tomb, for in the Fourth Gospel the body was already embalmed by Joseph and Nicodemus on the Friday. She was certainly special; how special is mostly mischievous speculation! She is never mentioned again in our scriptures – certainly not by Paul in his presentation of the resurrection narrative. But her encounter in John has led to the description of her as the 'apostle to the apostles'.[86]

It is clear that the stories featuring Thomas and Mary Magdalene are included in John's account of Easter to make his theological points: Jesus has gone away, Jesus has returned, Jesus is with us through the Spirit, intangible but real. The punch line to both stories is the blessing of those 'not seeing but believing' (20 v29); John's readers who were not there may receive the promise.

Postscript

There is another odd connection between Thomas and Mary Magdalene. They both appear in the titles of recently discovered so-called 'gospels'. The 'Gospel of Thomas' written in Syriac was unearthed in upper Egypt, where the sheer dryness of the atmosphere preserved so many papyri. It is a collection of Jesus' sayings rather than an account of his life, death and resurrection, so not properly a 'gospel' at all. There must have been several such collections, more or less authentic, depending on the memories of particular groups or individuals. Both Matthew and Luke drew on other sources to embellish Mark's Gospel. There is the 'Didache' from the early second century. Some scholars believe that the 'Gospel of Thomas' actually comes from the first century, i.e. as early as the Gospels, but most place it much later. Scholars are unsure on whether it was originally written in Greek or in Syriac; if the latter there is a link with Thomas if Syriac was his preferred language and the one he used in India. A fuller text (dated around 350 AD) was discovered in a Coptic translation. And not long after 350 Cyril, bishop in Jerusalem, could write: 'Let none read the Gospel according to Thomas: for it is the work not of one of the twelve Apostles, but of one of the three wicked disciples of Manes.'[87] It is thus one of several books which were never approved and were omitted from any canon of Christian scripture.

Similarly the 'Gospel of Mary' was rejected and only survives in fragments, sufficient for most to agree that the Mary in question is the Magdalene.[88] The various fragments were also discovered in dry Upper Egypt; scholars have provisionally dated them to the second century. The most fascinating section extant features Simon Peter asking Mary, in a very artificial dialogue: 'Sister, we know that the Saviour loved you more than the rest of the women. Tell us the words of the Saviour which you remember, which you know but we do not, nor have we heard them.' How unlikely is that! But the closeness of Mary to Jesus is again highlighted. The apostles respond in true male chauvinist spirit: 'But Andrew answered and said to the brethren "Say what you think concerning what she said. For I do not believe that the Saviour said this. For certainly these teachings are of other ideas". Peter also opposed her in regard to these matters and asked them about the Saviour. "Did he then speak secretly with a woman, in preference to us, and not openly? Are we to turn back and all listen to her? Did he prefer her to us?".' Did he indeed?

It is probably no more than coincidence that the two characters with the most distinctive roles towards the end of John are the two whose names are used to head up these so-called gospels. But it may point to the circulation of John's Gospel among the Jewish and Christian communities of Egypt, given that we know they were reading it by 125 AD. Rival or subversive groups, semi-Christian Gnostics, of which there were several in Egypt, when setting out to write up Christian teaching to suit their own interpretations and practices, would have found in John these two distinctive characters ideal to pin such documents on. Their efforts appear odd – and they are indeed odd – set against the measured and amazing text of John's Gospel itself. To paraphrase the closing phrase of the First Letter, 'Little children, keep yourselves from imitations!' (I John 5 v21).

Chapter 21

And Finally

No one reading John's Gospel could be in doubt that the final flourish of Chapter 20 vv30–31, was intended as the conclusion. What more remains to be said? And yet we have Chapter 21 in all the ancient manuscripts and, despite some quibbling among scholars, it seems to be an integral part of the book. It may thus be read as an epilogue to mirror the opening of Chapter 1, the prologue, though in a contrasting prose style with even a smile at the very end (21 v25).

There is a delicious theory that John or his scribe, having reached the end of Chapter 20, realised that there was quite a length of scroll remaining and decided to add this postscript because there was room for more! Maybe not. There are two episodes in this concluding chapter concerning the destiny of Simon Peter, plus what seems to be a comment on a debate at the time of writing. Like the fishing boat in verse 6, the chapter is full to overflowing with allusion and symbolism – yet does not quite capsize.

The first detail is the reprise of the story of Simon Peter's calling (Luke 5 vv1ff), enriched with allusions to other episodes, such as feeding the great crowd with bread and fish and Peter's walking on the water. John is drawing on the two strands of memories concerning the appearances of the risen Jesus. Luke and Acts place them all in and around Jerusalem, Matthew places them in Galilee. This extra Galilee episode seems odd in John, whose focus is on Jerusalem throughout, but clearly echoes what he has been told. Or it may be what the writer of this chapter experienced himself, as we shall see.

The seemingly miraculous catch is apparently counted. No one can be sure of the symbolism of the number 153 though it is most likely to signify the agreed number of the known peoples and tribes, i.e. the whole of humanity, the 'world' which God so loved. By the time of writing, the Christian message was well on its way around the known world. The miraculous catch is already happening and John's placing of this story, though less convincing than Luke's, does make the point. Jesus is again not quite recognisable, except to faith. It is the beloved disciple who says 'it is the Lord', the same one who ran with Peter to the tomb and 'went in and saw and believed' (20 v8). This is more than simple surprise; the uncertainty of recognition which is acknowledged in several resurrection stories is surely a pointer to credibility rather than fantasy. John intends it to be another example of not confusing physical with spiritual sight (20 v29).

The second scene develops the first. After the amazing catch is brought to land Peter is called by Jesus to 'follow me', this time not with the enthusiasm of a brand new fan as in Luke but in the cold light of day (albeit Easter day). The three-fold symbolism of the questions 'do you love me?' obviously mirrors the triple denial during that recent, dreadful night. It is very significant for John's readers, especially those who feel they too have failed. If Simon Peter could be forgiven and established as leader in the new church after what he had done, everyone might have hope and take heart. This final 'extra' chapter is an attempt to connect the amazing eternal truth of the story which concluded on such a high note in Chapter 20 with the everyday, workaday world where Christians like Peter needed to live out their faith, with its pressures, failures and fresh starts. Whereas the prologue sets the story of Jesus in a cosmic context, this epilogue is intentionally down-to-earth and, in its own way, reassuring.

Peter's martyrdom is foretold in the same language as that of Jesus, that it would be his death which would 'glorify God' (21 v19). This phrase on its own is sufficient to claim close kinship of this chapter with the evangelist who has been at pains throughout to describe the crucifixion of Jesus Christ as the moment of glory. The death of Peter is usually said to have been in Rome during the persecution under the emperor Nero in 64 AD though there is no independent testimony to that effect. He travelled after escaping from Jerusalem when Herod was persecuting the Christians, though he was back there in 50 at the celebrated council recorded in Acts 15. Perhaps he visited Corinth; there were 'followers of Cephas' there when Paul wrote his first Letter to the Corinthians around 55 AD (1 v12). Paul does not greet him with the others in Rome when he wrote his Letter to the Romans around 57AD. However, when Constantine erected a basilica in his honour in the 320s, the site was reportedly extremely difficult for building and was only chosen because of the revered location of the tomb of Peter, which recent archaeological research has supported, though of course not proved – we don't have any DNA from his relatives!

The final exchange between Jesus and Peter seems purely editorial, in that there seems to have been some controversy over the meaning of what Jesus said about the 'beloved disciple'. Had Jesus said that the End would come before he died? And now he was dead. The editor of this chapter is at pains to reassure his readers that this is not what Jesus meant. It is very difficult for us at this distance to get inside the minds of those first believers who awaited the End so urgently. For them this would be the moment when Christ would return in glory to establish judgement on the earth, the final transformation of earth and heaven, the vindication of believers and the overthrow of 'principalities and powers'. There has been much debate as to how the first Christians expected this End to come; we have seen that there is no suggestion of it in the earlier chapters of the Fourth Gospel. Such a belief might be echoed in the closing phrase of Revelation, 'even so, come, Lord Jesus', using the term Lord to signify the hoped-for overthrow of Rome (Revelation 22 v20). So to hear that something has happened which Jesus said would not happen before the End would have been alarming to those who believed that it would come soon; thus it would be well worth an addition to this chapter by way of reassurance. The editor of this chapter wants to dispel the rumour about the death of the 'beloved disciple' whom it is important to note is nowhere called John.

Which brings us to verse 24: 'This is the disciple who is testifying to these things and has written them, and we know that his testimony is true.' The first comment must be that 'the disciple who is testifying to these things' is not necessarily the 'beloved disciple', though it is logical to draw that conclusion from the succession of the verses. But we cannot be sure who the 'beloved disciple' was. It has been common practice to identify him with John the brother of James, and maybe that is right. But the Gospel does not actually say so. The description 'whom Jesus loved' does not appear until the accounts of the final days, starting with the exclamation of the crowd when Jesus weeps at the tomb of Lazarus: 'See how he loved him' (11 v36). This beloved disciple is present at the Last Supper in a favoured position; he is given charge of Mary by Jesus from the cross; he runs with Peter to the tomb where 'he saw and believed'; he joins the fishing party with Peter and recognises Jesus walking on the shore; and finally his death triggers John or his editor to re-interpret a saying of Jesus to reassure the church as to the end times. As to his identity, he has to be one of the fishing group (21 v2). He may or may not have been the 'other disciple' who knew his way round Jerusalem and could arrange for Peter's admission to the high priest's courtyard (18 v16). He was clearly a favourite of Jesus and in the Upper Room close enough to whisper a question to Jesus about the identity of the traitor on behalf of Peter who, for a mixture of emotions, dared not ask Jesus himself. Rather provocatively J. N. Sanders argues that the 'beloved disciple' was indeed Lazarus.[89]

The second comment is that 'this is the disciple who is testifying to these things and has written them' (21 v24) need not mean the actual writing. For example Paul normally dictated to a scribe or colleague, at least once signing off an epilogue in person (Galatians 6 v11). And 'these things' need not mean the whole of John's Gospel; it may be merely this final chapter. And yet clearly it cannot mean this verse (21 v24) if the 'beloved disciple' is dead. The reference may be a justification for appending this final chapter (perhaps written by the 'beloved disciple') to the Gospel which was written by someone else. Commentators debate these questions, review the options and then acknowledge that certainty is not possible. Thus Dodd writes 'the question of authorship is, on the basis of data presently available, incapable of decision'.[90] Nor does it matter overmuch. This Gospel is essentially commentary and interpretation of the phenomenon of Jesus of Nazareth; its authority does not derive from authorship but from impact. And as John would wish to point out, we are all 'beloved' disciples.

Then the Gospel ends on a most anti-climactic note, echoing and contrasting with his 'formal' ending (20 v31). Reiterating that this book only contains a selection of what might have been written, chosen deliberately to make a point, the writer signs off in a quizzical fashion, as much as to say: now go away and, through faith and love, fill the world with evidence that this is the truth sent from above.

Chapter 22

A Distinctive Message

So, to recap, what is this 'gospel according to John'? Despite the best efforts of preachers and church leaders, from the outset and continuing into the present century, the Christian faith as preached and lived is essentially a coalition of several approaches, rather than a coherent and consistent phenomenon – which would turn it into an ideology. In all authentic traditions the message and the faith are of course focused on the crucified and risen Jesus as Lord and Saviour. But already within the New Testament we can discern at least three emerging theological frameworks.

The struggle between Paul and the so-called 'Judaisers' is well known. They owed allegiance to James, called 'the Lord's brother', who was head of the Jerusalem church (Acts 15), not to be confused with James the son of Zebedee. His supporters wished to remain in effect a reformed version of Judaism and pursued Paul around the Mediterranean trying to subvert the inclusive gospel which he was preaching, a struggle recorded most graphically in his letter to the Galatians (e.g., Galatians 5 v12!).

John's approach is almost the opposite to that of James. It is hard to resist the view that this Gospel was primarily aimed at would-be Christians among the Jewish diaspora. Why would John make so much of his central message that salvation is recognising Jesus as the Christ, if his target audience did not know what a 'Messiah' was? But John certainly does not aim to win them over to a reformed version of their existing religion. Throughout the book each set-piece establishes how the new faith replaces the old. Each episode has, at least in part, that purpose, with cumulative points being made en route to the grand finale. All the bit-part characters with their dialogues, from Nicodemus onwards, develop the underlying premise that 'he came to his own and his own received him not' (1 v11). The eventual impact of chapter after chapter of growing antagonism between Jesus and 'the Jews' is inescapable. However awkward this is for us today – and it is very awkward – such an emphasis in John cannot be denied. Thus, while John may be 'the theologian', he cannot be the definitive theologian for us, especially in our contemporary relationships with Jews and Judaism.

So John's theology is not that of the 'Judaising' reformers; but it is also markedly different from Paul's. As we have seen their understanding of the death of Jesus is different, their understanding of the Holy Spirit is different, their interpretations of the 'end-times' are different (even though Paul does modify his earlier position) and the significance attached to the corporate life of the church as such is different. What constitutes salvation is differently expressed, though not the joy that it brings (compare 15 v11 with, for example, Romans 8). And for both the focus is firmly on grace, the initiative of God.

The Fourth Gospel is a distinctive strand in the evolution of Christianity in those formative decades. It is because we now read all four gospels and the other books in the New Testament as one volume that we cannot discern this distinctiveness without making an effort. For example, we saw how the familiar phrase 'Lamb of God' is automatically aligned with a doctrine of substitutionary atonement which is absent from John. Those who suppose that the whole of the New Testament fits together tidily must accept the challenge to clarify what they mean. And we are not helped by devotional books, lectionaries and liturgies which inevitably amalgamate all the strands. Present-day readers of John's Gospel, whether their church-going is regular or not, will inevitably blur their memories of the gospel stories being read. They may even expect John's teaching and testimony to fit into the framework provided by Paul's letter to the Romans (which William Tyndale called 'the principal and most excellent part of the New Testament'[91])! But it doesn't. John is different. It sometimes feels as though his whole message is directed to the self-confident 'elder brother' in Jesus' parable, while Paul is dealing with the 'younger brother' whose world had fallen apart (Luke 15 vv11ff). For today's reader John's core challenge, to move from a Jewish to a Christian faith, is hardly relevant; or it may appear as an invitation to anti-Semitism (that demonic 'light sleeper' as Conor Cruise O'Brien put it). But once that danger is acknowledged, there are riches here which every Christian needs, even if this book cannot stand alone as a primer of Christianity.

Even when John has Jesus at his most hostile to 'the Jews' in Chapter 8 there are lessons to be learned for our twenty-first century. This chapter is probably the least read aloud in church, as so much of it jars in a post-Holocaust age; when taken literally it is really difficult to follow. Here an angry Jesus sets out his stall and demands our attention, for John's target here is far beyond the Jewish crowd or leaders of Jesus' time. Hence even this passage has a powerful word for us. How hard it is for any people in any age, especially those hankering after a clear sense of personal or national identity, not to be the equivalent of 'children of Abraham' and blindly proud of it. For John there is a sinful pride in identity from which we need to be set free, a dark self-centred place which needs 'the light of the world' (8 v12). This is any narrow nationalism which lacks the awareness of being a 'citizen of the world', a human being. It is a gang mentality which follows the crowd, today on social media, back then by rousing the mob. If we now live in a 'post-truth' culture with 'alternative facts', with wily powerful Pilate as its patron saint ('what is truth?'), then what has happened to personal integrity, the hallmark of Jesus of Nazareth as he confronts Pilate and all that he represents? And what of the Servant King, given what John understands by costly coronation? Love defined as selflessness (12 v25) is a demanding struggle in any context, no less in our own. Those 'Jews' whom Jesus angrily confronts here and in some other angry exchanges are representative of all those of any race and religion who find ultimate value and corporate identity in their inner falsehoods sustained by 'false news', who build a rickety psychological or military scaffolding and call it security, who flaunt their spiritual deafness, who would rather blame victims than seek justice – all characteristics found in the Fourth Gospel and everywhere today. Surely this unlikely chapter is John's challenge to our own century of deal-makers and war-lords, and to our own complicity.

In the midst of which John offers good news. Bishop David Jenkins echoed John's message in his own personal credo: 'God is as he is in Jesus, therefore there is hope.'[92] Except that John would have concluded with 'life' – which is what David Jenkins means too. Despite some impatience and occasional anger, John's Jesus brings us a positive message. The divine Love goes ahead of us, watches our back and holds our hand, the same yesterday, today and for ever.

We do not see in the Fourth Gospel every facet of the faith, for no single presentation, biblical or contemporary, can offer that. We need to honour such diversity honestly. Christian unity is not just a matter of reconciling ecclesiologies (which has been the primary focus of the ecumenical movement) but of appreciating different and complementary approaches to the faith itself, given that the core is Christ Jesus. This is no simple spectrum, from conservative to liberal, 'literalist' to 'progressive'; but there is a necessary diversity as there has been since the first century. For his part, John is inviting us to accept that God does in fact love us and has demonstrated this in person, accepting us and even calling us friends, albeit as ineffective as the first twelve (15 v15). What Paul and others call redemption John calls victory, no less hard-won. With Jesus as Christ, the Word made flesh, believers are on the winning side in the ultimate struggle between light and darkness, good and evil, love and selfishness, life and death, yes and no. And John's deliberate preaching style forces his readers into a response; you may be moved by other Christian scriptures but you will be put on the spot (and hopefully changed) by John!

Chapter 23

From Beginning to End

The Good News Bible renders the opening two words of John's Gospel (*'en arche'*) as 'before the world was created'. But that is to miss the intention of John in intentionally echoing the opening words of the book of Genesis 'In the beginning' for John is not just chronological but existential. Because the term *'Logos'* or 'Word' means both a specific 'utterance' (as in: 'God said "let there be light"') and an underlying philosophical principle ('the generative and ordering principle of all that exists in the cosmos' as T. W. Manson puts it[93]) it is clear that John intends to set his story within the largest possible context. What happens in these chapters, he says, is the clue to the true meaning of life, the universe and everything (forgive the quote[94]).

Thus Jesus' climactic cry on the cross 'It is finished' is complex and profound for John. What is finished, accomplished, is not only the life of Jesus and the purpose of God for human salvation but the creation itself. This is foreshadowed in Chapter 17, 'I glorified you on earth by finishing the work you gave me to do. So now, Father, glorify me in your own presence with the glory I had in your presence before the world existed' (17 vv4f). The phenomenon of Jesus is the final clue, the definitive revelation of the nature of the creator. When Jesus is described by Pilate, 'behold the man!' (19 v5), had such a thing been possible John would certainly have written an upper-case M. There is nothing more to be said; the cosmic context of the prologue never quite goes away throughout the book. All our remaining years (what we used to call Anni Domini) are postscript, an interim period with the ultimate mystery already resolved. We now know why and how and who – we just don't know when!

We live in a time when the 'beginning' and 'end' of the

universe, of planet earth and of *homo sapiens* are being radically redefined by scientific discovery and theory. Thus there are fresh questions, including, for our purposes in this book, how far the time-expired elements of John's world-view will simply prevent our taking him seriously. There are many voices which describe religious belief, and the Christian faith in particular, as timeexpired, irrelevant and even dangerous. 'In the beginning' has now been chronologically determined, with some discernible version of the law of cause-and-effect operating ever since the earliest milliseconds after a 'big bang'. There may eventually be no gaps for the 'god of the gaps' to occupy! And as for the end, it appears that the phenomenon of the human race takes up little more than a few frames of a very long film. Despite the simplistic literalism of many believers, it is not very likely that the irresistible and total reign of God, with or without the rapture, will be coming to a planet near you any time soon. On the contrary, as John implies (in contradiction to the Book of Revelation) we are here for the long haul (17 vv15ff).

As we saw, the theologian and philosopher Leonard Hodgson outlines the authentic sequence of biblical interpretation, beginning with checking on textual accuracy, heading through what the author meant or intended, but always arriving at the vital question 'what must the truth have been if it appeared like this to people who thought like that?'.[46] And this is surely how John expected his readers to think, rather than (as more formal biblical commentators are obliged to do) spend all their time on the first stages. It has been the underlying purpose of this book to reflect on Hodgson's final stage, the good news of a knowable God.

John only uses the term *logos* in the prologue to the Gospel. It is his distinctive term and has stimulated a host of interpreters. But John, like all the New Testament writers, is seeking to commend rather than explain, to preach rather than theorise, to challenge rather than tease. He chose this term *logos* presumably because it would resonate with his intended readers. But he did not dwell on it or unpack it later (as he did the other prologue motifs of love and life, belief and rejection etc.) because he knew that such a debate might detract from the main message, the identity and trustworthiness of Jesus Christ. As with all theological language, *logos* is only a metaphor for revelation, after all. 'No one has ever seen God but God's only Son has made him known' (1 v18). This is what is meant by 'the *Logos* became a human being'. As in creation God has spoken. To describe Jesus as the incarnation of the *logos* of God is to invite every biblical scholar to wrestle with what is meant by that term; but that is not John's purpose. He is writing a gospel not a treatise, not even a theological one, whatever his reputation as 'the theologian'. The same comment applies to the spread of scholarly analysis of John's Gospel and its sources when compared with his contemporary life and culture. T. W. Manson has a strident paragraph:

The dogmas of the early Church are supposed to be derived from all kinds of sources – pagan mystery cults, late Greek philosophy, Hellenistic Judaism, Iranian redemption mysteries, and so on. The early Church, having selected one or more of these theories, then fitted Jesus into it! ... Rather it still seems to me much more likely ... that the Church began with the picture and tried to find a frame for it rather than that the Church first built an elaborate frame and then painted the portrait to suit. In other words the first Christians were Christians in the sense that they knew in their hearts that they owed their life to Christ.[95]

John the preacher is pressing his readers on Hodgson's final point 'how is all this true?', for my life, my attitudes, my prospects, and above all my relationship with God? The sequence of signs and dialogues is intended to draw his readers into an encounter with this knowable Son of God, to involve them in the story, to identify with one or more of his walk-on characters. That John drew on references to contemporary literature and culture is evident, even if the detail is not always clear, but it is always his intention that the message rises above its own time. He presents a sequence of very down-to-earth episodes, one-off encounters between Jesus and ordinary people, as of eternal significance, as 'signs'. This is a narrative device to draw the readers in and win them over. As we saw, many other faith traditions can accept that 'God chose Jesus' but John's whole message is that 'God chose to be Jesus'. To repeat, this is his acknowledged editorial purpose: 'Jesus did many other signs in the presence of his disciples which are not written in this book, but these are written that <u>you</u> may believe ...' (20 v30). This climactic use of 'you', meaning the general reader, is unique in all four gospels.

Whether John will persuade unbelievers is a perennial question for every generation and probably never more so than now. Are the arguments against faith in God so much stronger now than at other times? Maybe. Can the recurring failures of the Church and the flawed witness of Christians discredit the message itself for more than a single generation? Hopefully not, but also maybe. Will the dominant materialism of our times drive out a sense of 'other' and gradually close a gateway to John's interpretation of the phenomenon of Jesus as God's Word made flesh and the lives of believers as testimony to God's living Spirit? When the sound has died away, will the music still be heard? Shall we 'have the experience but miss the meaning', as T. S. Eliot puts it?[96] Will all the answers to 'how' eventually drive out the last 'why'?

There are sadly several reasons for supposing that today's circumstances and culture are more likely to sustain doubt and that such doubt may more readily become acknowledged disbelief than in previous times. The fact that these reasons (intellectual and emotional) derive from a materialism which its advocates are struggling to reinvent for this 'quantum' age is not a strong enough defence; general inexplicability has never been a proper argument for the existence of God! With typical robustness, Marilynne Robinson puts the case: 'The human sense of the sacred is a fact. ... It is a given, a powerful presence, whose reality it is perverse to deny on the basis of a model of reality constructed around its exclusion.'[97] Yet this denial is now the default stance, even in a century when the very meanings of time and of matter are becoming ever more mysterious.

It is as true today as it has ever been that when sceptics want to 'see the mark of the nails in his hands and place their finger in the mark of the nails' (20 v25) they will not be granted Thomas' experience nor any other knock-down argument of a more general nature. There can be no proof; this Logos is not logical like that. And yet, and yet ... in the end, which is what John means by 'in the beginning', there is in his Gospel a declaration of a divine purpose and love, once embodied in Jesus Christ, transcending all other threats or promises, an offer finalised by victory on a cross, an invitation which will never be withdrawn, in time or beyond. Reader, you'd better believe it!

Appendix

Notes and References

All the Bible quotations are from the New Revised Standard Version (Anglicized Edition), Oxford University Press 1995. The name 'John' is used to signify the author of the Fourth Gospel throughout, making no assumption as to his identity.

Chapter 1

1. Eusebius (265–340 AD), *Ecclesiastical History* (EH) III, 39. Of course, all this tells us is what was reportedly believed in the Roman Province of Asia in the second century. There is much debate among scholars as to whether Papias, always assuming that Eusebius is quoting him correctly, is a reliable commentator on the link between Mark and Peter. This well-known passage from Eusebius is used by C. E. B. Cranfield (*The Gospel According to St Mark*, Cambridge 1959, p. 3f) who comments: 'This is a quotation within a quotation and gives us the testimony of an older contemporary of Papias who is probably to be identified with the Elder John.' This Elder, John, is himself one of the 'prime suspects' as author of John's Gospel but, as we shall see, this does not imply that this John wrote his Gospel after reading Mark's.

2. C. H. Dodd, *The Interpretation of the Fourth Gospel*, Cambridge 1953, p. 6, hereinafter referred to as 'Dodd, *Interpretation*'.

3. Clement was a Christian teacher in Alexandria in the late second century. Among his works was 'Outlines' (*Hypotyposes*), now lost, from which Eusebius claims to have taken this quote (EH VI, 14).

4. C. H. Dodd's other great work on this Gospel is *Historical Tradition in the Fourth Gospel*, Cambridge 1963, hereinafter referred to as 'Dodd HT'.

5. Dodd, HT, p. 413; he continues: 'For this conclusion I should claim a high degree of probability – certainty in such matter is seldom to be attained.'
6. See Dodd, HT, p. 17, after several pages of discussion he continues: 'But in fact the question of authorship is not as important for the problem of historicity as has been supposed.'
7. Dodd, HT, p. 431.
8. C. H. Dodd, *The Founder of Christianity*, SCM Press 1999, his last book (written at the age of 85). Someone joked when it came out, 'not another book about Paul!' given Dodd's lifelong study and interpretation of the apostle to the Gentiles.
9. John Marsh, *The Gospel of St John*, Pelican New Testament Commentaries, Penguin Books 1968, p. 81.

Chapter 2

10. As in Matthew 12 vv46ff, where Jesus actually says 'who is my mother and who are my brothers? ... whoever does the will of my Father in heaven is my brother and sister and mother'. In Luke the contrast is even stronger: when a woman in the crowd shouts 'blessed is the womb that bore you and the breasts that nursed you!' Jesus replies 'blessed rather are those who hear the word of God and obey it' (Luke 11 v27). So much for the 'blessed' Virgin Mary, one might think!
11. In 19 v26 the NRSV has 'here is your son' where the Greek literally has 'see' and other versions 'behold' which is surely better.
12. Dodd, *Interpretation*, p. 395.
13. 3 v17; 5 v30; 8 vv15f; 12 vv44ff.
14. There is a long-running and passionate debate around what might constitute a good society in a much less religious age. First up was Alasdair MacIntyre *After Virtue* (University of

Notre Dame Press, 1981). One contemporary commentator is the former Chief Rabbi Lord Jonathan Sacks: 'So what do I mean by religion in the public square? I mean simply religion as a consecration of the bonds that connect us, religion as the redemption of our solitude, religion as loyalty and love, religion as altruism and compassion, religion as covenant and commitment, religion that consecrates marriage, that sustains community and helps reweave the torn fabric of society' (*speaking in* New York on July 13, 2017). But these are not John's concerns.

15. Exodus 3 vv13ff where the Hebrew has YHWH, translated in the NRSV as 'I AM WHO I AM' and usually transliterated as Yahweh or The LORD. This is 'the name that is above every name' (Philippians 2 v9).

Chapter 3

16. Lewis Carroll, *Through the Looking-Glass and What Alice Found There*, Macmillan, 1871.

17. Dodd, *Interpretation*, p. 208, footnote. On the main page he comments: '... the action in which He fully expressed Himself, namely his self-devotion to death in love for mankind, is the conclusive manifestation of the divine glory. In developing this thought, the evangelist plays subtly upon the varying meanings of the word *doxa* suggesting that by such a death Christ both "honours" God (by complete obedience) and gains "honour" Himself; but the "honour" which He gains is none other than the "glory" with which the Father has invested Him.'

18. J. N. Sanders (with B. A. Mastin), *The Gospel According to St John*, A & C Black, 1968, p. 82.

19. Brian Wren's hymn 'Great God, your love has called us here' can be found in several collections, e.g., *Rejoice and Sing*, 339.

Chapter 4

20. Dodd, HT, p. 423.
21. Paul refers to this in I Corinthians 16 vv1–4 and reflects on it throughout II Corinthians chapters 8 and 9, where he pleads for generosity, holding up the churches in the north of Greece (Macedonia) as examples.
22. Dodd, HT, p. 245.
23. Dodd, HT, p. 67; Dodd is very impressed by this (see Chapter 22 of this book).

Chapter 5

24. This book, originally published in 1894, is newly available in paperback through wordery.com.
25. Dodd, *Interpretation*, p. 313.
26. William Temple, *Readings in St John's Gospel*, Macmillan 1968, p. 149. The Times Literary Supplement reviewed this book: 'This will take a high and honoured place among the best devotional literature … (It) is worth a dozen of the ultra-modern critical studies to which in recent years we have sometimes been subjected.'
27. In Mark 14 v62 Jesus responds to the High Priest with allusions to Daniel: 'Again the high priest asked him, "Are you the Messiah, the Son of the Blessed One?" Jesus said, I am; and "you will see the Son of Man seated at the right hand of the Power" and "coming with the clouds of heaven".'
28. 'Prosperity Gospel' describes a strand of preaching which ascribes wealth as the will of God and the fruit of faithfulness. It has been linked to 'tele-evangelism' and several high-profile 'charismatic' leaders, though a version of this theology goes back to E. Kenyon in the nineteenth century. In the latter half of the twentieth century preachers like Oral Roberts, Kenneth Hagin, Gordon Lindsay and Matthew Ashimolowo have popularised this message. The approach has been disputed from within evangelicalism and

by leading Pentecostalists, as well as by most mainstream church leaders and teachers.

29. Marsh, p. 376.

Chapter 6

30. Dodd, *Interpretation*, Part 1 *passim*.

31. Scholars are not agreed on the relationship between the First Letter and the Gospel. They mostly agree that the Gospel writer did not write the Second and Third Letters, still less the Book of Revelation. Dodd's conclusion is that 'the simplest hypothesis seems to be that the author of the Epistle was a disciple of the Evangelist and a student of his work ... not a mere imitator' (*Moffatt Commentary on The Johannine Epistles*, Hodder and Stoughton 1946, p. lvi). But it was not unknown for extracts from known apostolic writing and thought to be adapted and enlarged by a dutiful editor to make a new work, with claimed apostolic authorship – and authority. For example, this seems to be the case with the Letters to Timothy and Titus which are ascribed to Paul. Thus, as Dodd implies, the First Letter of John may well have much from the mind and the teaching of the Gospel writer, albeit rewritten and edited. But, as he also says (ibid. p. liv), '(as for) Eschatology, the Atonement, the Holy Spirit ... in all three the First Epistle of John represents an outlook widely different from that of the Fourth Gospel'.

32. *Commentary on the Epistles*, p. 31. The First Letter is more self-consciously addressing the Christians who have taken up with Gnosticism, heretics who claim a knowledge of God. Here Dodd offers a helpful outline (pp. 29–32) touching on the Platonic and Old Testament origins of this controversy around 'knowledge of God'. As he writes, 'In this passage (I John 2 vv1–6) our author is not only rebutting dangerous tendencies in the Church of his time but discussing a problem of perennial importance, that

of the validity of religious experience. ... But unless the experience includes a setting of the affections and will in the direction of the moral principles of the Gospel, it is no true experience of God in any Christian sense.' In *Interpretation*, pp. 97–114 Dodd offers a longer overview of Gnosticism, including this comment 'no general and all-embracing answer can be given to the question "what is the relation of Gnosticism to Christianity?"'.

33. It must never be forgotten how little we 'know' (as *savoir*) of God, given that we are invited to know (as *connaître*) God through Jesus. Marilynne Robinson (*The Givenness of Things*, Virago Press, p. 189) has unearthed a splendid quotation from John Locke: 'what a darkness we are involved in, how little it is of Being, and the things that are, that we are capable to know ... (we must) sometimes be content to be very ignorant'. (*An Essay Concerning Human Understanding* vol. 2, book 4, chap.3, p. 222)

To which one would say with Dr Robinson, 'Amen and amen'. This whole essay, *Metaphysics*, is full of the spirit, and sometimes the words, of John's Gospel, not least when she writes: 'I suppose it is my high Christology, my Trinitarianism, that makes me falter at the idea that God could be in any sense repaid or satisfied by the death of his incarnate self' (op.cit. p. 194).

34. Philip Pullman, *The Good Man Jesus and the Scoundrel Christ*. Thus Wikipedia *(autumn 2017)*: 'Published in 2010 by Canongate Books, as part of the Canongate Myth Series, it retells the story of Jesus as if he were two people, brothers "Jesus" and "Christ," with contrasting personalities; Jesus being a moral and godly man, and his brother Christ a calculating figure who wishes to use Jesus' legacy to found a powerful Church.'

Chapter 7

35. Sir Herbert Butterfield (1900–1979) was Regius Professor of History and Vice-Chancellor of the University of Cambridge. He wrote *Christianity and History* (Bell, 1950) from which Wikipedia offers a couple of quotes:

    'If there is a meaning in history, therefore, it lies not in the systems and organizations that are built over long periods, but in something more essentially human, something in each personality considered for mundane purposes as an end in himself.'

    'I have nothing to say at the finish except that if one wants a permanent rock in life and goes deep enough for it, it is difficult for historical events to shake it. There are times when we can never meet the future with sufficient elasticity of mind, especially if we are locked in the contemporary systems of thought. We can do worse than remember a principle which both gives us a firm Rock and leaves us the maximum elasticity for our minds, the principle: Hold to Christ, and for the rest be totally uncommitted.'

36. T. S. Eliot, 'Little Gidding', published in 1942, final section. This poem, the fourth and final one in *Four Quartets*, speaks of love as purification or destruction: 'We only live, only suspire / consumed by either fire or fire.' Commentators note that Eliot was intent on the need for a costly fresh start for society. 1942 also saw the publication of the Beveridge report anticipating the fresh starts in economic and social policy that would be needed after the war. The theme of starting afresh runs through John's Gospel which it is fascinating to read alongside 'Little Gidding'.

37. Dietrich Bonhoeffer, *The Cost of Discipleship*. This was the first of his books to be published in English in 1948 in an abridged version and then in full (with a moving Foreword from Bishop George Bell) by SCM Press in 1959. In German the title is simply *Nachfolge*, meaning 'following', published

in 1937 and in the main a commentary on the Sermon on the Mount. By then Bonhoeffer and his colleagues in the Confessing Church already knew what might happen to them under Hitler, as indeed it did. In this powerful book he writes of ‚cheap grace' as the preaching of forgiveness without requiring repentance, and of costly grace which 'confronts us as a gracious call to follow Jesus. It comes as a word of forgiveness to the broken spirit and the contrite heart. It is costly because it compels a man to submit to the yoke of Christ and follow him. It is grace because Jesus says: "My yoke is easy and my burden is light"'.

38. Lesslie Newbigin, *The Light Has Come – an exposition of the Fourth Gospel*, Eerdmans, 1982. As it says on the cover, this is 'strictly an exposition, seeking to interpret the text to contemporary human beings, not a scientific critical commentary nor a series of devotional meditations'. Much like this little book, then!

Chapter 8

39. Paul's Letters are often structured in two parts, first teaching about the faith, then his teaching or instructions about its implications. Hence one of his favourite little words, 'therefore', appears at Romans 12 v1, Galatians 5 v1, Ephesians 4 v1, Philippians 4 v1, Colossians 3 v5.

40. This promise is somewhat puzzling if not daunting. Most commentators assume that John is referring to the multiplication of Christ-like love by so many followers of Jesus when the Holy Spirit comes. Thus William Temple, for example: 'In scale, if not in quality, the works of Christ wrought through His disciples are greater than those wrought by Him in His earthly ministry. It is a greater thing to have founded hospitals all over Europe and in many parts of Asia and Africa than to have healed some scores or some hundreds of sick folk in Palestine.' Temple, p. 227.

41. Marsh, p. 184.

Chapter 9

42. What is usually called 'Second Isaiah', chapters 40–55, contains several references to this Servant including 41 v8, 42 v19, 43 v10, 44 v1 and 49 vv3ff. The main reflection on suffering as the mark of the Servant comes in Chapter 53, prefaced by 52 v13ff.
43. Verse 2 of Charles Wesley's hymn 'Spirit of truth, essential God'.
44. Sydney Carter in *'The Present Tense'* © Galliard 1968.
45. Dr C. I. Scofield, with a group of mainly American fundamentalist scholars, produced an edition of the Authorised Version, published by Oxford in 1909 'with a new system of connected topical references to all the greater themes of scripture, with annotations, revised marginal renderings, summaries, definitions, chronology and index, to which are added helps at hard places, explanations of seeming discrepancies and a new system of paragraphs'.
46. Leonard Hodgson, *For Faith and Freedom* (Gifford Lectures 1955–1957), SCM Press, 1968, p. 87.
47. John M. Campbell, *'Being Biblical'*, United Reformed Church, 2003, p. 18, quoting Albert Schweitzer, *'The Quest for the Historical Jesus'*, in English, A & C Black, 1910, p. 4.
48. Rowan Williams, *Holy Living*, Bloomsbury, 2017, introduction.

Chapter 10

49. Sanders p. 462, quoting Augustine *On marriage and concupiscence* II,6.
50. Sanders comments (p. 460) that 'it is usual to regard (it) as a piece of floating tradition'. One manuscript places it after Luke 21 v38, where Jesus is teaching in the Temple. Sanders quotes the distinguished commentators Westcott and Hort

(from 1881): 'Had he *(the scribe who places it in Luke)* known it as part of a continuous text of St John's Gospel he was not likely to transpose it.'

51. The corresponding noun 'salvation' is often used by Luke, five times each in the Gospel and in the Acts. It appears frequently (along with the related words 'Saviour' and 'saved') in the Letters of Paul and in the rest of the New Testament, though never in Matthew or Mark.

Chapter 11

52. This is what he said in a broadcast interview. Professor Dennis Nineham wrote in David Jenkins' obituary in *The Guardian*, 'He referred to the resurrection being "far more than a conjuring trick with bones", which was widely misquoted. This was far from being a gaffe; on the contrary it was an act of great courage, for it was part of a deliberate policy of bringing into the open the problems besetting religion in the late 20th century. "I want," he said, "to get them talking about religion in the pubs." He succeeded. Yet any disquiet his words caused in the diocese was largely dispelled by his palpable devotion to essential Christian faith, including a quite traditional understanding of the incarnation, and by his caring pastoral approach.'

Chapter 12

53. Today's settlements on the West Bank and in the Gaza strip, though declared illegal by international courts and the UN, are viewed by many settlers as fulfilments of scriptural prophecies. Here are two: 'The Lord will roar from Zion and thunder from Jerusalem; the earth and the heavens will tremble. But the Lord will be a refuge for his people, a stronghold for the people of Israel. Then you will know that I, the Lord your God, dwell in Zion, my holy hill. Jerusalem will be holy; never again will foreigners invade her' *(Joel 3:16-*

17), and 'I have posted watchmen on your walls, Jerusalem; they will never be silent day or night. You who call on the LORD, give yourselves no rest, and give Him no rest till He establishes Jerusalem and makes her the praise of the earth' (Isaiah 62:6–7). These two quotations are prominent on the pro-settlement web site http://free.messianicbible. com/feature/gods-promises-an-inheritance-for-israel-and-the-settlements/

Chapter 13

54. Temple, p. 184.

Chapter 14

55. Dodd, HT, p. 62.
56. *Judas*, Amos Oz, Chatto & Windus, 2016.
57. Sanders has a fascinating paragraph, p.18; he writes 'The relative value of Mark and the Fourth Gospel ... presents a remarkable analogy to that of Xenophon and Plato for the understanding of Socrates', and he develops this theme.
58. Dodd, *Interpretation* , p. 230ff; this is an extended section examining the various interpretations for the unique phrase 'Lamb of God'. 'I conclude that the expression "the Lamb of God" in its first intention is probably a Messianic title virtually equivalent to "the King of Israel", taken over by the evangelist from a tradition which also underlies the Apocalypse of John. It is possible enough that other ideas may be in some measure combined in it, for our author's thought is subtle and complex' (p. 238).
59. C. S. Lewis, *Surprised by Joy*, Fontana, p. 178.

Chapter 15

60. It was a familiar style in ancient philosophical writing to set out as dialogue what is in fact a treatise. The best-known examples are in Plato's 'dialogues' which are dramatised

dissertations.

61. Dodd, *Interpretation*, p. 395.

62. Dodd, *Interpretation*, p. 397.

63. One might compare the past tenses in the Magnificat (Luke 1, 46ff) which express the timeless confidence of faith.

64. Dodd, *Interpretation*, p. 398.

65. Wikipedia reminds us (*autumn 2017*): 'The *Filioque* is included in the form of the Niceno-Constantinopolitan Creed used in most Western Christian churches, first appearing in the 6th century. It was accepted by the popes only in 1014 and is rejected by the Eastern Orthodox Church, Oriental Orthodox Churches and Church of the East.' This word and the dispute over its use in various documents get two substantial Wikipedia entries!

66. Charles Wesley's 1746 hymn begins: 'Away with our fears, our troubles and tears; the Spirit is come, the witness of Jesus returned to his home' and is in many collections, e.g., Rejoice and Sing, 323.

Chapter 16

67. This interpretation is from George Caird lecturing at Mansfield College Oxford in 1964, when he was attending the Second Vatican Council as a *'peritus'* biblical scholar and as a representative of worldwide Congregationalism. The present writer recalls a twinkle in his eye as he said it.

68. A recent review of Churches Together in England does acknowledge that this is now recognised by many as a shift in ecumenical thinking over recent decades: 'On a broader level, it is fair to say that the traditional models of ecumenism, with top-down structures, and formal dialogues between professionals within hard denominational structures has increasingly given way to a more relational, action-orientated and grass-roots form of ecumenism.' *That they all may be one*, report from Theos, circulated by Churches

Together in England as a free download, October 2017.

Chapter 17

69. Dodd, *Interpretation*. The first 130 pages of this book deal with the background of the Fourth Gospel, but always with this premise: 'The fact is that the thought of this gospel is so original and creative that a search for its "sources" or even for the "influences" by which it may have been affected, may easily lead us astray' (p. 6).
70. Newbigin, p. 181f.
71. Thus Wikipedia (*autumn 2017*): 'In 597, Augustine and his companions landed in Kent. They achieved some initial success soon after their arrival. Æthelberht permitted the missionaries to settle and preach in his capital of Canterbury. ... In the early medieval period, large-scale conversions required the ruler's conversion first, and Augustine is recorded as making large numbers of converts within a year of his arrival in Kent.'
72. See also Rowan Williams, *Faith in the Public Square*, Bloomsbury, 2010, chapter 10.

Chapter 18

73. Cannibalism, resulting from a misunderstanding of the 'supper of the Lord', was just one of the charges aimed at discrediting the Christians across Roman society. Professor Robert Louis Wilken has several examples in *The Christians as the Romans Saw Them*, Yale University Press, 1984.
74. Sanders, p. 402.

Chapter 19

75. Dodd, HT, p. 67.
76. Sanders, p. 380.
77. J. H. Newman's words are taken from his lengthy poem 'The Dream of Gerontius' written in 1865; these verses were

first used as a congregational hymn as early as 1868 and are in most hymn books. The original poem uses 'Praise to the Holiest in the height' as a refrain five times to begin each section; the oratorio by Elgar only uses these few verses once, with a recapitulation at the end of the work.

78. Wikipedia *(autumn 2017)* summarises: 'In the early 2nd century AD, the site of the present Church had been a temple of Aphrodite; several ancient writers alternatively describe it as a temple to Venus, the Roman equivalent to Aphrodite. Eusebius claims, in his *Life of Constantine* (written 200 years later), that the site of the Church had originally been a Christian place of veneration, but that Hadrian had deliberately covered these Christian sites with earth, and built his own temple on top, due to his hatred for Christianity.'

79. *Itinerarium Burdigalense*, p. 594.

Chapter 20

80. The Travels of Marco Polo, Book 3, Chapter 18; in the translation of Henry Yule (Courier, 1871). There are fascinating anecdotes in this chapter about Thomas' resting place and its miraculous powers, such as: 'The Christians who go thither in pilgrimage take of the earth from the place where the Saint was killed and give a portion thereof to any one who is sick of a quartan or a tertian fever; and by the power of God and of St. Thomas the sick man is incontinently cured.'

81. Marsh, p. 646.

82. Pliny the younger was the Roman governor of Bithynia; he wrote a letter to Emperor Trajan around 112 AD asking for advice on dealing with Christians. *Epistulae*, X.96.

83. C. H. Dodd, *Studies in the Gospels*, pp. 18ff quoted in HT, p.148.

84. Temple, p. 363.

85. In her radio drama *The Man Born to Be King*. Thus Wikipedia *(autumn 2017)*: 'It is a play cycle consisting of twelve plays depicting specific periods in Jesus' life, from the events surrounding his birth to his death and resurrection. It was first broadcast by the BBC Home Service on Sunday evenings, beginning on December 21, 1941, with new episodes broadcast at 4-week intervals, ending on October 18, 1942. The series was written by novelist and dramatist Dorothy L. Sayers.'

86. The title was used from early times, most precisely by Saint Thomas Aquinas in his commentary *In Ioannem Evangelistam Expositio, c. XX, L. III, 6.* More recently Pope Francis has honoured her as reported in *Vatican City, July 22, 2016*: 'Faithful to the wish of Pope Francis, a new decree has bumped the liturgical celebration honouring St. Mary Magdalene from a memorial to a feast, putting her on par with the apostles.' The reason, according to Archbishop Arthur Roche, is that she 'has the honour to be the first witness of the Lord's resurrection'. 'She is the witness to the risen Christ and announces the message of the Lord's resurrection just like the rest of the Apostles,' he said, explaining that for this reason 'it is right that the liturgical celebration of this woman should have the same rank of Feast as that given to the celebration of the Apostles in the General Roman Calendar.'

87. Cyril, *Catechesis*, 6. 31.

88. See Wikipedia entry 'Gospel of Mary', detailing the textual and interpretative issues.

Chapter 21

89. Sanders, pp. 30ff.

90. Dodd, HT, p. 16.

Chapter 22

91. William Tyndale: *A prologue upon the Epistle of Saint Paul to the Romans*, opening sentence.
92. This was described by James Bell (at David Jenkins' funeral on September 28, 2016) as 'one of David Jenkins' great affirmations, often and justly quoted. ... This one statement knocks on the head the nonsense of "the unbelieving Bishop"'.

Chapter 23

93. T. W. Manson, *On Paul and John*, p. 139. This short book is one of the splendid Studies in Biblical Theology published by SCM Press in the 1960s, now apparently only available through the American distributor LOGOS as a set, though individual volumes may be found online.
94. A phrase derived from '*The Hitchhiker's Guide to the Galaxy*' by Douglas Adams, first on BBC radio 1978. Deep Thought (the all-powerful computer) speaks after seven and a half million years: '"The Answer to the Great Question ... Of Life, the Universe and Everything ... Is ... Forty-two," said Deep Thought, with infinite majesty and calm.'
95. Manson op. cit. p. 156.
96. T. S. Eliot, *The Dry Salvages*, in *Four Quartets*.
97. Marilynne Robinson, *The Givenness of Things*, Virago, 2015, p. 241. Dr Robinson has received many accolades as a novelist and essayist. She has recently been elected a Fellow of Mansfield College Oxford.

CHRISTIAN FAITH

Circle Books explores a wide range of disciplines within the field
of Christian faith and practice. It also draws on personal testimony
and new ways of finding and expressing God's presence in the
world today.
If you have enjoyed this book, why not tell other readers by
posting a review on your preferred book site.

Recent bestsellers from Circle Books are:

I Am With You (Paperback)
John Woolley
These words of divine encouragement were given to John Woolley
in his work as a hospital chaplain, and have since inspired and
uplifted tens of thousands, even changed their lives.
Paperback: 978-1-90381-699-8 ebook: 978-1-78099-485-7

God Calling
A. J. Russell
365 messages of encouragement channelled from Christ to two
anonymous "Listeners".
Hardcover: 978-1-905047-42-0 ebook: 978-1-78099-486-4

The Long Road to Heaven
A Lent Course Based on the Film
Tim Heaton
This second Lent resource from the author of *The Naturalist and the
Christ* explores Christian understandings of "salvation" in a five-
part study based on the film *The Way*.
Paperback: 978-1-78279-274-1 ebook: 978-1-78279-273-4

Abide In My Love
More Divine Help for Today's Needs
John Woolley
The companion to *I Am With You*, *Abide In My Love* offers words of
divine encouragement.
Paperback: 978-1-84694-276-1

From the Bottom of the Pond
The Forgotten Art of Experiencing God in the Depths of the
Present Moment
Simon Small
From the Bottom of the Pond takes us into the depths of the present
moment, to the only place where God can be found.
Paperback: 978-1-84694-066-8 ebook: 978-1-78099-207-5

God Is A Symbol Of Something True
Why You Don't Have to Choose Either a Literal Creator God or a
Blind, Indifferent Universe
Jack Call
In this examination of modern spiritual dilemmas, Call offers the
explanation that some of the most important elements of life are
beyond our control: everything is fundamentally alright.
Paperback: 978-1-84694-244-0

The Scarlet Cord
Conversations With God's Chosen Women
Lindsay Hardin Freeman, Karen N. Canton
Voiceless wax figures no longer, twelve biblical women,
outspoken, independent, faithful, selfless risk-takers, come to life
in *The Scarlet Cord*.
Paperback: 978-1-84694-375-1

Will You Join in Our Crusade?
The Invitation of the Gospels Unlocked by the Inspiration of Les
Miserables
Steve Mann
Les Miserables' narrative is entwined with Bible study in this book
of 42 daily readings from the Gospels, perfect for Lent or anytime.
Paperback: 978-1-78279-384-7 ebook: 978-1-78279-383-0

A Quiet Mind
Uniting Body, Mind and Emotions in Christian Spirituality
Eva McIntyre
A practical guide to finding peace in the present moment that will
change your life, heal your wounds and bring you a quiet mind.
Paperback: 978-1-84694-507-6 ebook: 978-1-78099-005-7

Readers of ebooks can buy or view any of these bestsellers by
clicking on the live link in the title. Most titles are published in
paperback and as an ebook. Paperbacks are available in traditional
bookshops. Both print and ebook formats are available online.

Find more titles and sign up to our readers' newsletter at
http://www.johnhuntpublishing.com/christianity. Follow us on
Facebook at https://www.facebook.com/ChristianAlternative.